T0058335

MEDITATIONS
for
BUSY MOMS

MEDITATIONS
for
BUSY MOMS

REFLECTIONS, SCRIPTURE, AND WISDOM

SANDRA DRESCHER-LEHMAN

Good Books
New York, New York

MEDITATIONS FOR BUSY MOMS

Good Books books may be purchased in bulk at special discounts for sales promotion, corporate gifts, fund-raising, or educational purposes. Special editions can also be created to specifications. For details, contact the Special Sales Department, Good Books, 307 West 36th Street, 11th Floor, New York, NY 10018 or info@skyhorsepublishing.com.

Good Books is an imprint of Skyhorse Publishing, Inc.®, a Delaware corporation.

Visit our website at www.goodbooks.com.

10 9 8 7 6 5 4 3 2 1

Library of Congress Cataloging-in-Publication Data available on file.

ISBN: 978-1-68099-201-4
eBook ISBN: 978-1-68099-202-1

Cover design by Jane Sheppard

Interior images courtesy of iStockphoto

Printed in China

To John,
my husband,
and the most wonderful
partner in parenting
I could ever want.

And to Claire,
Godmother to our children
and my "angel,"
who on many occasions
has relieved the burden of my weariness.

About This Book

I wanted to write this book for quite a while, but life with young children does not leave energy to spare. Raising children takes nearly all the creativity one can muster and quite a bit of self-forgiveness for what cannot be mustered.

As I finally began to write, I thought of how universal "weary parenting" is. The two words naturally go together, but the "weary" part is often lived in silence and without the benefit of support from others. As long as I act like an energetic, self-contained parent, those are the only kind of parents I meet. When I admit that I'm tired and am not sure how to take the next step, my friends disclose their doubts, fears, and frustrations to me also. Meeting at that point of honesty, we give each other a boost back into the creative, loving, and pleasurable (or at least tolerable) arena of parenting. We lend each other patience and understanding as we confess our questions and weariness together.

May this book be a support for you during those alone moments of weary parenting. May the thoughts and feelings that you allow yourself to admit and accept heal the pain of being less than perfect. May you, in turn, bless others who need to hear that to parent in a state of exhaustion is to be normal.

— Sandra Drescher-Lehman

Sleep-Deprived

I wonder what it would be like to go to bed in the evening, knowing that I could sleep all night without being on call for bad dreams or puddles in the bed. I used to have that, but I didn't know how wonderful it was then, and now I forget.

I wonder what it would be like to lie down in the middle of the day and take a nap. I used to be able to do that, but then I didn't want to, and now I can't remember why not.

I wonder what it would be like to sleep as long as I wanted, into the bigger hours of the morning. It was called "sleeping in," I think. I wonder, do people still do that?

God, I'm so tired.
Help me to sleep deeply
in the hours I do have,
to lie down in peace.

I lie down and sleep; I wake again,
for the LORD sustains me.

—Psalm 3:5

Adding Up the Little Things

"What did you do today?" I knew Joanne wasn't calling to keep tabs on me or to condemn what I didn't do. She was genuinely interested in finding out what was happening with me.

"I'm not sure," I heard myself say, "but I don't remember sitting down all day and I'm exhausted." What have I done all day? That's hard to answer when I'm trying to prove myself worthy of the time I have, especially when all I can think of is that I played games and read books with my children, made meals, cleaned up messes, took walks, answered questions, plus a myriad of other little things.

I know they all add up. I also know these are the little things that are the important parts of life! They just don't brag well if you insist on listing your accomplishments.

**God, I know you think my day
was well spent with my children.
Help me to remember the value of those moments.**

You, O LORD, are a shield around me, my glory,
and the one who lifts up my head.

—Psalm 3:3

Time-Out

Today I raised my voice above all the noise and fighting I could no longer bear and announced that I was going to Time-Out. I marched straight to my bedroom, closed the door, and took 10 deep breaths. I breathed into my neck and shoulder muscles to relax them, and tried to remember that I'm the one who's supposed to be in control here.

I was in control when I opened the door again and left my mini solitude. It was a good thing I was, because my children weren't. My announcement had scared them, and they were waiting quietly to see what had happened. Maria whispered, "I didn't know parents can go to Time-Out!"

I had recovered enough calmness to explain that Time-Out is not a punishment; it's a break in what's happening so energy can be redirected.

Everyone needs Time-Out sometimes. The next time I hope my children will better understand its use and not be frightened by it—their Time-Out or mine.

**It takes but one intentional moment
to change the atmosphere.**

Create in me a clean heart, O God,
and put a new and right spirit within me.

—Psalm 51:10

Worn Out

When I look at my two little children, I wonder how they can wear me out so completely. I wonder how my sister, with twice as many, keeps going.

I recently asked my mother, who raised five, how she did it. She said that now she knows she was in a state of exhaustion for twelve years straight. Then she couldn't afford the time or energy to think about it.

Maybe that's the time my sister is in now. And maybe I'm not as tired as I could be, since I obviously have the time and energy to realize how worn out I am. That's a scary thought!

Either way—I'm tired.

Lord, may being aware of my weariness
help me find the rest I need.

Return, O my soul, to your rest,
for the LORD has dealt bountifully with you.

—Psalm 116:7

Naps

Rachel told me one time that when her children go down for a nap, her feet go up. She renews herself by closing her eyes or reading a book.

I've thought about that a lot. I think it's a wonderful idea. I just have a few questions. First of all, how do you get everyone to sleep at the same time? Second, when do you get the last meal cleaned up and the next one started if it's not at nap-time? And third, can you really relax with toys all over the house, or do you at least clean up the space where you want to sit?

I had to find out, so I went back to Rachel with my questions. She said, "Well, that was an ideal situation I was talking about! It doesn't happen every day."

Now that I understand. It's good to have wonderful goals and to also know they won't always be met.

**God, help me remember my goal
of carving out little bits of time for myself.
Help me be content with
attaining that goal every once in a while.**

Be transformed
by the renewing of your minds.

—Romans 12:2

Dealing with the Unexpected

How could he do that? How could he go and break his arm when I need that arm?

After the panic of getting his bike home and him to the hospital emergency room, I began to face the reality about what that cast meant for my life. This was not in our plans.

I want to be a sympathetic and caring wife, and I know John's not overjoyed about breaking his arm either. But all I can think of is how I'll be stuck doing ALL the cooking and cleaning and laundry now, instead of sharing the jobs. I can't tell him my feelings, though. I certainly can't say them out loud.

Many women do all the housekeeping and child-rearing. I grant that I am spoiled to have a husband at all, and to have one who doesn't assume all the housework is mine to do. Right now, though, I'm worn out just thinking about what lies ahead.

**Thank you for listening to my anger
at this unexpected intrusion, Lord,
because I can't tell anyone else.**

Listen to the sound of my cry,
my King and my God,
for to you I pray.

—Psalm 5:2

Piles

Piles happen so fast, I'm convinced they have a life of their own. I can't decide what to do with the mail, so I stick it on the pile to look through later. I have forms to fill out, but no time, so they land on a pile. I have a pile of recipes to try, letters to be answered, and books I'd like to read. Another pile begins to form—of stickers and doll clothes and an assortment of toys.

I finally blow up! "No more piles. This place is a mess. Today we will go through our piles and find homes for everything."

At the end of the day, I notice that my children's piles are gone. I notice that most of mine are still there- one in the dining room, one in the kitchen, one in the den, one in the living room, one in the bedroom, and one on the stairs.

I ask Julie, who never seems to have a pile in the house, how she does it. She said her piles are all in her bedroom with the door closed. That beats having to look at a pile in every room of the house.

Later I find out what happened to my children's piles. They simply carried them to their rooms.

**Watch them; your children may be able
to teach you some things!**

And a little child shall lead them.

—Isaiah 11:6

Creativity

Last week Jane took me to visit a woman she thought I'd enjoy meeting. When we arrived, the woman was working in her art studio, a room lined and piled high with her work. Music was bouncing from the walls.

The lyrics and melodies penetrated my soul as I walked among her projects, and I felt a familiar excitement. It was a world of creativity much like I had once inhabited. I used to thrill at the inspiration that would appear in a moment of solitude.

Now I feel creative when I follow a recipe for a batch of playdough and tint it two different colors. I think I'm doing well if I get clean clothes back into everyone's drawers. I'm lucky if I remember to turn on music!

Then I noticed that there were no children in this woman's studio. Soon enough my life will have no children running around in it, demanding my attention.

It was a moment of grace—remembering the creativity I once had, the creativity it takes to raise children, and the creativity that will be mine again when the time is right.

Lord, give me patience and perspective.

Restore us to yourself, O LORD, that we may be restored;
renew our days as of old.

—Lamentations 5:21

Creativity Revisited

We went back to Jane's house where her three children were busy playing games with mine. She mixed up a pitcher of lemonade for them and then cheerfully began making dinner for all of us.

While she went to the garden to dig potatoes, pick a few beans, and gather some herbs, I explored the shelves in her tiny kitchen. I discovered spices and oils I didn't even know how to pronounce. Not surprisingly, her dinner was soon producing delicious, unfamiliar smells, as she sprinkled a variety of seasonings into different pots.

The meal Jane served that evening opened my eyes to another kind of creativity. Cooking is one of those things most parents must do, but I can choose whether I'm going to open cans and simply heat up our meals, or use some of that creativity I was saving for later. I can nurture anticipation for mealtimes in my children, and we can all feel rich together.

That sounds so wonderfully ideal. I could at least try it once a week for starters.

Thank you, God, for inspirations.
Help me to keep dreaming big.

You have put gladness in my heart
more than when . . .
grain and wine abound.

—Psalm 4:7

Off the Record

Before John left for work this morning, he asked what I had planned for the day. "Not too much," was my thoughtless reply.

So when he got home this evening it was fair of him to ask, "Did you have a relaxing day?" It was fair, but it hit me cold. Relaxing? That's about the last word I would have chosen.

True, this morning I couldn't think of much I had to do, but this much I know: I didn't stop all day—mending hearts I didn't know would break, cleaning up messes I didn't plan to have, answering phone calls I didn't know were coming, making lunch for the friend who dropped by unexpectedly with her children at 11:45 a.m., running to the library with the books I forgot were due yesterday, and wiping up more messes.

No, it was not a relaxing day. It was an exhausting day. It's good I didn't have much to do.

**Thank you for your guidance
through unplanned territory.**

For you bless the righteous, O Lord;
you cover them with favor as with a shield.

—Psalm 5:12

Be Extravagant

Sharon emailed me today, thanking me for remembering her fortieth birthday. She wrote that she was having a hard time with the thought of being that old, so her husband gave her forty roses.

Forty roses! I'm having a hard time being this old, too. I wonder if my husband knows that? I'd be happy with one of any kind of flower, for that matter.

It reminds me of a woman I worked with years ago. She didn't wait around wishing that someone would send flowers to her. She often bought a bouquet for herself and graced our office with it.

I think I'll do that for myself today. I'll go buy myself a flower, one that smells good and looks elegant and reminds me that there is goodness in life and that I may absolutely enjoy it. Maybe I'll buy a flower for a friend, too.

**Lord, help me love myself
the way I know I need it.**

O Lord, our Sovereign,
how majestic is your name in all the earth!

—Psalm 8:1

Phone Calls

Why is it that when someone calls, that's the exact moment one of my children needs me? From the time they were babies, the phone's ringing seemed to be their cue to start crying.

Now they can talk. They don't always talk. In fact, they can play contentedly for long periods of time. Let the phone ring, however, and they immediately need my attention—right away!

My friend calls from work a lot, just to chat. I've noticed she never calls from home when she's with her children. She wonders why I don't take any initiative in our friendship and call her sometimes. Maybe if I had a full-time job outside our home I would.

For now, I refuse to be on any committee that requires making a lot of phone calls. I want my children to know they are important to me.

**Strengthen me, Lord,
for the refuge I know
my children seek from me.**

Let me abide in your tent forever,
find refuge under the shelter of your wings.

—Psalm 61:4

Cleaning

I was talking to a couple of friends recently. One has four grown children and the other has no kids. Both women said they set aside one day a week for cleaning their houses.

I was shocked. First of all, if I knew I was going to clean all day, I doubt that I could get out of bed that morning. More importantly, I realize that I forget other people spend time cleaning, too. Of course I know it in my head. But it is such a lonely thing to do that when I'm in the middle of it, I imagine all the things my friends are doing, and it's never cleaning! They're going to parks or having lunch with each other or reading books to their children.

I'm relieved to know other people do spend time cleaning. Even if some have cleaning women, they still have to clean up for their hired help! My weariness does love company.

Thank you, God,
for the comfort of knowing
that I'm part of a huge community
of housekeepers.

In all toil there is profit.

—Proverbs 14:23

Melted

I am extremely grateful that John was not working late tonight. I was ready for my shift to be over when he walked in the door at 5:30. One more minute with these kids and my exhaustion would have exploded into a whiny tantrum—the kind I tell them they must learn to control.

After dinner was finally over and cleaned up, the toys put away, and the last load of laundry folded, I slumped into the chair across from where John was reading to our children. I watched and wondered how I could have gotten so frustrated with them earlier. Tears from the day's pain were dried and long forgotten. The dirt collaring their necks had been washed away. Instead of throwing marbles down the stairs for the sheer joy of noise, they were curled up cozily beside their dad, soaking in his words and love.

I felt love building back up in my heart. I hadn't lost it, but it had taken some time to be rekindled. When my son looked over at me, my feelings oozed out onto my face. And then the best gift of all—he smiled back. I melted.

**Thank you, God,
for the possibility of calm moments,
and especially for the times when they happen.**

Just as water reflects the face,
so one human heart reflects another.

—Proverbs 27:19

Simple Picnic?

When Ann called earlier this week and asked if I wanted to have a picnic in the park with our children, I eagerly agreed. It sounded like a great idea.

When the morning finally arrived, however, it took all my energy and coordination to get us out of the house on time; well, close to the right time! I couldn't think of anything to match the nutritious lunch I knew Ann would bring. I grabbed an opened bag of pretzels, hoping they weren't stale, and tried to remember if there was a water fountain at this park.

What a relief it was to get to the park first, and then to see Ann pull up with lunches from McDonald's! I'm grateful for a friend who helps me relax about not being perfect.

**Thank you, God,
for vitamins.**

My times are in your hand.

—Psalm 31:15

Yikes—Gray Hair!

I'm not old enough for this! I can't believe my hair is turning white already. Okay, maybe it's only gray, but still . . .

At first I thought it was just the light shining on it in a weird way, but that delusion didn't last long. One closer look and I knew it was the beginning of my end.

I was warned that having children could do this to me. But I thought it came as a result of parenting teenagers. Think what I'll look like by then—their grandmother.

I have options, don't I? Coloring has its pros and cons. I wonder if my friends are getting gray yet. I bet a high school class reunion would do me good about now. I could also simply accept this as another stage in my life—of growing maturity, perhaps! I think I'll begin by working on my attitude about all this.

**Change is more certain
than remaining unchanged.**

Gray hair is a crown of glory;
it is gained in a righteous life.

—Proverbs 16:31

Read and Read

I'm too old for this job! My knees hurt when I bend down to reach my child, and my back hurts when I try to get up again. Once around the bases wears me out (if I'm lucky enough to get a hit), and just thinking about soccer makes me long for a nap. An hour inside a box playing house, even though it is a big box, is much too long. Pretending to be a baby puppy is worse.

Maybe this is why I read so much to my children. Even when they each beg for a different book, reading is still easier for me when I'm tired than playing their games. I think it's about time for another trip to the library.

Thank you, God,
for helping me to think of options
when I'm too tired to move.

I will satisfy the weary,
and all who are faint I will replenish.

—Jeremiah 31:25

Super Ball Syndrome

I just figured it out! It came to me during the fourth task Maria asked me to do simultaneously!

First, she wanted me to help her sew a pillow for her doll. I was proud of her stroke of creativity; I thought a pillow would be a fun project to work on together. However, as I was looking for the cotton stuffing and my sewing box she saw a book she wanted me to read to her. So we sat down and read for a few minutes. Then she asked to listen to a tape and wondered if I'd sing along with her. Two songs into the tape, she wanted a snack and wondered why I hadn't finished her pillow yet.

I felt like a Super Ball that had just been bounced all over the house. Did Maria feel as out of control as I did?

I'm going to have to make a conscious effort not to let myself unravel totally. It's not too early to help Maria learn to do one thing at a time. I wish I would have learned it before.

**Help me to slow down
and make conscious decisions
instead of being driven
by every request that comes along.**

Better is the end of a thing than its beginning.

—Ecclesiastes 7:8

A Good Kind of Tired

I'm tired tonight. I'm bone-weary, muscle-sore, heart-happy tired. Being tired isn't new. But being worn out because of something concrete I did gives me a feeling of satisfaction I don't usually get from being with kids all day.

Our children went to a friend's house for the afternoon, and John and I took the rare opportunity to go for a bike ride. I felt the joy of the open road again. And I remembered the times B.C. (Before Children) when we would ride eighty to one hundred miles a day and camp out along the road at night, so we could get up and do the same thing the next day.

Today's fourteen miles have worn me out to the same degree as those longer rides once did. I may not be used to this kind of demand anymore, but my body and soul have loved the ability to meet it!

**Being tired
and feeling like I deserve it
is a state of weary ecstasy!**

I will both lie down
and sleep in peace.

—Psalm 4:8

Gift of Smell

I love the smell of my son's sweaty body. I love the chance to cuddle his warm, worn-out self close to me and remember together all that made our day full and rich. There is not a single weary soul at the end of today, but two. I have worked hard at being a parent, and he has worked hard at being a child.

In our peaceful snuggling, I realize that when he no longer wears me out, I will no longer have the chance to breathe in the smell of his sweat so closely. The arms that work for him, also get to cradle him. The legs that run with him endlessly, also get to push the rocking chair where I hold him, now quiet on my lap. The mouth that tries to keep up with all his "Why" questions, also gets to say, "I love you."

This sweaty body holds the memories of his busy day. And for now, he lets me hold him—close.

**Thank you, Lord,
for smells that give an immediate reminder
of the beauty of life.**

Ah, the smell of my son is like the smell of a field
that the LORD has blessed.

—Genesis 27:27

Overheated

It's too hot today to move any muscles. When I have to do anything, my body feels like it's creeping in slow motion. I want nothing more than to lie under a fan with a wet handkerchief over my face. (I'm looking for that option in my job description.)

Children don't notice the heat. They fly around, repeatedly drag dirt into the house, want more snacks, stub their toes, and cry for the part of the popsicle that fell in the sand.

The most creativity I can muster today is to get into their little plastic pool. The blessing of the day is that no one stopped by while I was sitting in six inches of water with them, fully dressed!

**Some days,
survival is the best I can do.**

He who sits in the heavens laughs.

—Psalm 2:4

Time to Relax

I got up at 9:30 this morning and was on the couch sleeping again by 1:30! Grandma was cleaning up lunch dishes and had gotten out games for my children. I woke up later, then drifted back into dreamland while the kids happily chattered and organized Aunt Karen's stuffed animal collection. I remember trying to figure out why I was so sleepy and being a little embarrassed that my relatives would think I'm always this lazy. The next thing I knew, I was waking up an hour later.

Slowing down for the four-hour drive to Grandma's house gave my body a chance to relax and feel how tired it had become, a fact I usually don't have the luxury of considering. I wish for every parent these kind of weekends at the in-laws—minus the embarrassment.

**Take a well deserved rest
every chance you get!**

The beloved of the Lord rests in safety . . .
the beloved rests between his shoulders.
—Deuteronomy 33:12

Mondays

It's Monday again. Ugh. After the fun of being with my family and friends all weekend, working, playing, and relaxing together, the return of routine is downright cruel. I'm suddenly alone. My children are around, as are the pets, but I'm alone when it comes to bearing responsibility for whatever happens here.

I was so busy last week getting ready for the weekend that I never got around to planning for today. The only way I seem to be able to make it through a Monday is to plan for at least one little upper, like buying some good coffee or going on an outing to the library. I don't need much, but I have to be intentional. Otherwise, I'll be wallowing in the Monday blues without realizing why, and we all know who gets the brunt of that. The children.

**Know the times
you are most prone to feel down;
then make plans
to be good to yourself.**

May he grant you your heart's desire,
and fulfill all your plans.

—Psalm 20:4

Positive Energy

I try to be honest. If a friend asks me how I'm doing, I hurry my brain to revive memories of the last twenty-four hours so I can tell them how it's been. Never mind that their "How are you?" was more politeness than a true inquiry.

Lately my answer to that question usually comes out on the negative, fatigued side, and I take some satisfaction in sharing my misery. It helps to a certain extent.

This week, however, has been good. I've gotten more sleep than usual, I've thought of things to cook, and I've had some satisfying times with friends. So when people ask "How are you?" I've actually said, "I'm great!" I got an extra lift just hearing myself say that. I've discovered I can be as happy getting attention from being positive as from confessing my exhaustion—maybe more.

I think I'll try this alternative response, even when it's not totally true. Maybe focusing on the goodness I have will be a pervasive and positive influence on how I am.

**Thank you, God, for the times,
few though they be, when I do feel very good.**

Come and hear, all you who fear God,
and I will tell what he has done for me.
—Psalm 66:16

Whining

"People need loving the most when they deserve it the least." A little plaque engraved with these words jumped out at me from my sister-in-law's wall. Why did that remind me of my child?

I had a very hard time feeling my love for her yesterday. In fact, I didn't feel it at all. She whined about not having her favorite cereal. She begged to buy candy at the store. She complained when I turned the TV off after two shows and launched from there into a tirade of "Why can't I have more videos?"

I got some reprieve when she went to a friend's house to play in the afternoon, but she was more whiny than ever when she returned home and discovered the rules were still the same—like, "Pick up your own toys!" Her behavior did not deserve love.

But then, why should my child be any different than me? I whined to John all evening about our ungrateful child. It seems I need loving, too, when I deserve it the least.

Thank God, I don't get what I deserve!
Teach me how you do it, Lord.

The LORD will fulfill his purpose for me;
your steadfast love, O LORD, endures forever.
Do not forsake the work of your hands.

—Psalm 138:8

Saving Energy

Call me old-fashioned. Call me ridiculous. The truth is, when I woke to the sound of raindrops this morning, I was excited. The laundry basket is piled high, and rain means that I will have to use the dryer instead of hanging the wash on the line, which would be the financially and ecologically correct thing to do.

Nobody is standing over me with an account of how much electricity I waste, but I feel it in my bones, my very responsible bones, my overly responsible bones. Most people don't seem to have these kinds of bones. Most people can freely use the dryer even when it's not raining. I wonder if most people are, therefore, less worn-out than I am.

Well, I'm not most people, but I suppose I can treat myself sometimes to one of the luxuries of housekeeping—the dryer!

**Learn to recognize the difference
between real and self-inflicted burdens.**

Come to me, all you that are weary
and are carrying heavy burdens,
and I will give you rest.

—Matthew 11:28

Is It Really Vacation?

I remember that before we had children, vacations were actually relaxing. I sort of wish I didn't remember, though, because I'm sure that's why I got irritated last week.

Children don't vacation like I want to. In fact, our vacation was pretty much like being home, only more work. We didn't have the conveniences of our own cupboards, our favorite foods, washing machine, or beds. The drive was too long and the proximity of the car's inhabitants too close.

I long for the days when I could drive for miles in silence. I remember when vacation was for catching up on magazines. I felt energized at the end. Now vacation has completely worn me out. I need to go back to work to recuperate.

What I really need is to redefine vacation before it redefines me.

**Help me, Lord,
to enjoy each stage of my family's life.**

Do not say,
"Why were the former days better than these?"
For it is not from wisdom that you ask this.
—Ecclesiastes 7:10

Take a Break

I loved having contact with another adult in the middle of the day. I hadn't realized how full of kid details my head was until I got a break from them.

I was a better mother when I came back to my children, having talked to another parent about how difficult our job is. I wasn't as annoyed and surprised, then, at my kids' interruptions during the rest of the day. I recognized the importance of comforting yet another tear-stained face instead of trying to make him be brave and strong. I saw that my children, too, were tired after dinner, and I was willing to help them get to bed instead of hurrying through my own chores first.

I think I'm being a full-time mother, but I'm really trying to take care of them and take care of me at the same time. Meeting my own social and emotional needs today for a couple of hours helped me be present to the children when I returned. I intend to plan times away more often.

**Thank you, God,
for the perspective a good break provides.**

The LORD is my shepherd . . . he restores my soul.
He leads me in right paths for his name's sake.
—Psalm 23:1, 3

Give a Break

It seems I'm not the only one who can benefit from a break. I'm finding my children can be healthier with some time away from me as well. Of course, they recognize their need as little as I usually do my own.

Jonathan cried when I left him with my sister and her family for several days and begged me not to go. By the time I left, I couldn't remember, either, why I had to spend some time alone with my husband.

When I returned, however, I knew why it was important. We were refreshed again in our marriage. My five-year-old met me with the biggest smile and hug I had ever gotten and a proud, "We did it!" Later, he said, "Aunt Rose yells just like you—only louder." I told him that's because she's younger. Secretly I was glad he had learned that I'm not the only mother who gets upset. Other mothers yell, too, and it never means we don't love our children. Our time apart cemented that fact deeper than ever in both of our hearts.

**Thank you, God,
for extended family and friends
who give my children a broader base of security.**

Whoever does the will of God
is my brother and sister and mother.

—Mark 3:35

Light a Candle

Symbols are important teaching tools for me. That, together with the fact that I have an aging memory, prompted me to light a candle today. A friend asked me to remember her because she was anticipating a hard day, so the burning candle was for her.

I put it on the table in the middle of the house so that every time I walked through the room, I was reminded to pray enlightenment into her spirit. In the middle of the cries and demands of my household, the flame called me to pray peace into her day.

At the end of the day, I felt like I had given something to the world. The candle helped me live beyond my own little space and care for another. That simple act energized me! I'm sure I have another friend for whom I could light a candle tomorrow.

**Thank you, Lord, that even on the days
when I don't get out of the house,
you can use me for a bigger purpose
than my own family.**

Command the people of Israel
to bring you pure oil of beaten olives for the lamp,
that a light may be kept burning regularly.
—Leviticus 24:2

Strengthening Ego

Today I noticed Constance, a friend of mine, stoop down to my daughter's level and say, "I just want to tell you, you have a beautiful smile." Maria didn't say a word, but her response was overwhelming. She looked at Constance and broke into a huge smile. My own body glowed with the kind of warmth that I felt sure was spreading through Maria as well.

For me, it wasn't pride in having a daughter with a beautiful smile. It was the warmth of another adult noticing her, going out of her way to tell her she was special. It was an affirmation of her life.

Her comment also gave a boost to my parenting job. I know I can't be everything for my child. I need an extended family and friends who help to strengthen her sense of self.

As Maria soaks affirmation into her soul, she will have more to give to others. The value of my friends to my children cannot be demanded or measured. I simply watch with deepening gratitude.

**God, thank you for friends
who help me raise my children.**

Your right hand has supported me;
your help has made me great.

—Psalm 18:35

Mentoring

After experiencing the wonder, yesterday, of another adult blessing my child with affirmation, I remembered other times that has happened. I thought of Jessica, their babysitter, who asked if she could take the children out to their favorite park one day—not for pay, but because she loved them. I thought of Joanne asking Maria to "do nails" with her and her girls. Just last week Scott took her window-shopping when Maria was clearly bored being with me. Claire often stops by with magazines, stickers, or cards that she knows my children will love, or to play a game with them.

Being grateful for the others who put effort and love into the lives of my two reminds me to do that for other children—and their parents. Many of us live far away from grandparents, brothers, sisters, and cousins, whom we may naturally count on to love our children.

I need others to be role models and mentors for my kids. They also need me to do the same for their children.

**Help me, God,
to put out a little more energy
when I think my children are taking it all,
to let other children know they are special.**

Let the light of your face shine on us, O LORD!

—Psalm 4:6

Reality Isn't So Bad

Usually everyone's happier when friends come over to play. Everyone's busy and no one needs me as much.

Today was definitely not one of those times. Each of my kids had a friend here, and I spent the entire afternoon putting on bandages, tying shoes, cleaning paint out of clothes, wiping dirty hands and faces, washing a trail of sticky popsicle droplets from the kitchen, through the dining room, and down the hall, washing the deck of spilled cups of lemonade (after I finally got smart enough to send them outside), and trying to convince the boys that the girls, screaming as if pain-ridden, were really only covered with red paint.

My saving grace was a friend who stopped by, stepped into the middle of the chaos, and broke up laughing. I had failed to see the humor. When I stopped long enough to see her pleasure, however, I was brought to reality—the reality of how much fun the children were having, the reality of how fortunate I am to have the time to have my children's friends come play at our house, the reality of having a family.

**Help me, Lord, to renew my appreciation
for the gifts I have in my home.**

Then you shall see and be radiant;
your heart shall thrill and rejoice.

—Isaiah 60:5

Caffeine

I caught myself this morning saying, "I need my cup of coffee." Sounds bad.

Bad because if I do consider it "my" cup of coffee, then I'm likely addicted. It's no longer simply a drink of pleasure or a small comfort. Instead, I need it to function.

The truth is I am a better person after I've had a cup of coffee. I could do without it, although I'd rather not. I don't enjoy the ensuing headaches.

I wondered what parents do who don't like coffee. I asked the only two I know. Julie admitted that she has to have "her" Pepsi every day and Carmen has "her" chocolate.

Most of us parents need a little extra energy from somewhere. I'm not too nervous about being addicted. When I start to spell "my" or "coffee" with a capital letter, I'll consider cutting back.

**Thank you, God,
for creating the coffee bean!**

My flesh and my heart may fail,
but God is the strength of my heart
and my portion forever.

—Psalm 73:26

Bloom Whenever Possible

There's a mix-up in my backyard. It's September and the tips of my lilac bush are in bloom. I'm feeling mixed up, too, right now, but in reverse. I'm supposed to be blooming but I'm not.

I'm supposed to be joyful about caring for my children, but I'm too tired to recognize the gift they are to me. My life is supposed to be enriched by sharing it with children, but they leave me feeling depleted. I'm supposed to be full of creative ideas that will bring out the best in their growth; I'm pleased with myself if I get clothes in their drawers and closets that simply keep pace with their growth.

Maybe one of these days I'll bloom unexpectedly, like my lilacs. I'll quit worrying about what I'm supposed to do and just bloom when it comes, no matter how brief or irregular the moment.

**Watch for the petals of joy
that can infiltrate
even a tired mind and body.**

Consider the lilies of the field,
how they grow.

—Matthew 6:28

Pets

I like having animals. I really do. I grew up on a mini farm, where I learned to value the fun and responsibility of having pets. I don't want living in the city to deprive my children of the lessons to be discovered from God's creatures. On a good day, I think it's great that we have a dog, a cat, two hamsters, a frog, a turtle, and 24 goldfish.

This, however, is not a good day. Where was my mind when I agreed to all this? (I actually never agreed to the cat and the turtle; they just came and stayed.) I feel run out of my own house. All I want is some solitude—not a dog breathing on me or a hamster running on a squeaky wheel or a cat finding my lap as soon as I sit down. The fish are even irritating me. They swim toward me with their mouths open every time I walk past. It's enough to wear anyone out.

Actually, I was worn out before this day started, just thinking about all I have to do to get ready for my parents' visit this weekend. My kids better not ask for a bird again today!

**Perceptions can change radically
in the heart of the weary.**

The earth is the LORD's and all that is in it,
the world, and those who live in it.

—Psalm 24:1

Resolving Conflict

My friend Joy mentioned today that her evenings are taken up with figuring out how to help her kids get along. I hadn't put that activity into words before, but I share the experience.

I hate to hear one of my two getting hurt, so my immediate impulse is to jump on the other one. I know it's better to let them, or help them, work it out themselves, but my ability to do that depends on my energy level. It's often easier to separate them or just say, "STOP IT!" Now who's yelling?

What really irritates me is that by the time I choose sides, they're giggling together again. I'm slowly learning that emergencies, for which I need to respond quickly, do happen. Squabbling siblings, however, rarely constitute these emergencies. If I can let them learn to resolve conflict with each other, they will be able to use those skills for the rest of their lives, with all the others with whom they will interact.

**Help me, Lord,
to remember the long-term goals
of raising my children.**

And now faith, hope, and love abide,
these three; and the
greatest of these is love.

—1 Corinthians 13:13

Little "Helpers"

It's all I can do not to express my impatience when the dishwater is lukewarm and splashing all over the counter and floor, the five-minute pile of dishes has already stretched into fifteen minutes . . . and the dishes are only half done.

I have to literally bite my tongue so I don't yell about the flour that's flying all over the floor and the chairs and into the drawers, after I suggested that making cookies together would be a good project.

It's hard to repeat calmly, three times in a row, "That's enough spray on your dust cloth."

Theoretically, letting children help with chores is a great idea. That's the only way they will learn, of course. Eventually, their help may even save time. I'm having a hard time imagining that now, however, when their help increases my workload.

**Help me to remember how many wet bellies
my parents let me have at the kitchen sink.**

Let the little children come to me;
do not stop them;
for it is to such as these
that the kingdom of God belongs.

—Mark 10:14

Death

My six-year-old called me to his room. He was sitting on the edge of the bed and burst into tears when I appeared.

"I don't want you to die," he blurted out. "I'd be too sad." What could I say? That I won't die? I wanted to comfort him, but I couldn't lie.

Finally, "I'm not planning to die any time soon. Why are you worried?"

"Because you're older than me."

"That doesn't mean I'll die soon or first."

"Well, I don't want to die first either! Then you'll be too sad."

"It would be nice if we could both wait a long time and then die together, wouldn't it?" I wasn't sure, when the time came, that we would want that option either, but it seemed like the right thing to say.

We sat there hugging and crying, and he was soon comforted enough to move on to his next thoughts and games, apparently. I was left, however, with the awakened thought that I could die and leave my children without a mother. I needed someone to hold me and let me cry, and then remind me that today, right now, I'm very alive.

God, I don't mind begging.
Please let me live to help my children grow up.

So do not worry about tomorrow, for tomorrow will bring worries
of its own. Today's trouble is enough for today.

—Matthew 6:34

Announced Silence

I'm glad my children can talk now. I like knowing that he's crying because his ear hurts or that she's grouchy because she has a headache. I especially love it when they verbalize thoughts like, "I love you."

Talking has its other side, though, too. Sometimes I simply can't listen to one more question. I find myself saying "Uh-huh" when I notice the monologue has paused for a response. I can't believe my four-year-old caught me doing that today. I was zoned out from him, and trying to follow directions to a new store, when I heard from the back seat, "No, Mommy. The answer is NO!"

I wasn't fooling anyone with my pseudo-attention. These are the moments when I have to initiate the Silent Game. We see who can be quiet the longest. Children seem to deal with silence that is announced, better than being obviously ignored.

**When your attention span
has reached its limit,
teach your children
how to take a break with you.**

Let me have silence,
and I will speak.

—Job 13:13

Parent Power

I was amazed by what my friend was saying. It was sharing time on Sunday morning. Traditionally, this was a time to ask forgiveness of the community if necessary, but nobody does that much anymore. We mostly ask for prayers for our friends and family or share the things we're happy about.

This woman, however, was telling us that she had abused her power as a parent. She had used force against her child and wanted us to pray that she would be forgiven and get her behavior under control.

After the service, I rushed to her side to let her know she is not alone. I was going to tell her of the time when out of my own exhaustion and anger, I threw my child into bed because she wouldn't stay there and take a nap! By the time I reached my friend's seat, she was already surrounded by other parents making similar confessions.

Since that day, I know that I'm part of a community of people who are willing to acknowledge our power and work together not to misuse it. I carry our shared struggle in my heart and use its strength when my own is gone.

Power carries much responsibility.

In you, O LORD, I seek refuge;
do not let me ever be put to shame;
in your rightcousness deliver me.

—Psalm 31:1

Imagine Alternatives

I'm looking at my kids today thinking, "When are their parents coming to pick them up?" Their clothes and toys are scattered all over the house and I'm too tired to care.

I'm too tired to think of anything to make for dinner. I'd just as soon set aside this day for a family fast.

I'm too tired to sort the dirty clothes into lights and darks. I've changed my mind about our sanitary needs. We can all wear these clothes again tomorrow. Well, maybe not the youngest, now that I look at him.

I'm too tired to help them, or to insist that they pick up their toys. But if they don't, maybe I'll step on some quite by accident, and then I can just throw them away. That would save a lot of time, now and in the future.

I must be resigning myself to remaining their mother. I seem to be imagining alternatives for living in this state of exhaustion. I'd like to dream a little longer though: "When are their grandparents coming to pick them up?"

**Recognize alternatives,
even if they're only good for a laugh.**

Do not close your ear to my cry for help,
but give me relief!

—Lamentations 3:56

Life on the Edge

I feel fragile today—frighteningly fragile. If one more person asks me to do something, or spills milk on my papers, I will tip right over the edge of sanity into whatever lies beyond. It's too scary to think about that outcome, so I hold onto myself, one arm wrapped across the other arm as if someone bigger than me were here.

As simple as that sounds, it helps. It reminds me that I'm not alone. There is Someone bigger, inviting me back from the edge, soothing my spirit. Someone is whispering that spilled milk is natural and not a natural disaster, but maybe I should move my papers. And I can choose to which demands I will respond, rather than playing puppet to every suggestion.

Yes, I'm living on the edge today. It's nice to know I'm not alone, although it feels that way.

When the storm pushes you to the edge,
take a step backward,
for balance and perspective,
and wait it out.

But you do see! Indeed you note trouble and grief,
that you may take it into your hands;
the helpless commit themselves to you.

—Psalm 10:14

Feeling Fragile

Feeling fragile is not comfortable. It doesn't seem to fit with being a parent. Feeling fragmented to the breaking point was bad enough when I was alone, but now I'm responsible for these little, dependent people who look to me for their physical and emotional safety. I can't curl up in the overstuffed chair and hug myself all day.

Expecting more of myself than I have to give, however, adds an additional layer of weariness. Maybe on days like this I'll choose the couch, so there's room for all of us to cuddle up together. We can read books. I need to ease back and my children need my shelter. Reading Pooh stories about the warm, fuzzy bear of little brain, will work quite well today.

**Nurture yourself
along with your children.**

O LORD my God,
in you I take refuge.

—Psalm 7:1

Making Space

I have an image that helps me through moments when I feel close to shattering. I imagine there are flowers blooming in the center of my being. All my favorite ones are there in a mixture of yellow, orange, pink, and purple, my favorite colors.

When too many people make demands on my time and energy all at once, I feel like the world is pushing in on me and my flowers are getting crushed. I feel like dandelion tops look when a two-year-old brings them to me in his tight fist.

So I breathe deeply and pull in air for my flowers. I expand the space where they are and push the pressure back out to the world. I imagine them spreading out their petals and leaves again, relaxing in the new air.

It's amazing what goodness a few deep breaths can bring to my soul. Help me, Lord, to remember to care for my flowers.

**What do you nurture
at the center of your being?**

The vines are in blossom; they give forth fragrance.
Arise, my love, my fair one, and come away.
—Song of Solomon 2:13

Going Strong

Today I'm strong. I'm not sure what makes the difference between a fragile day and a strong day, but on days like this, I don't waste much time wondering. I just enjoy what's happening.

Today my children could scream and run as hard as they want and, every once in a while, I might calmly ask them to turn it down a notch. They could say they hate everything I put on the table to eat and I would still know that I'm a good cook. They could even disrespect me without making me question my worthiness.

Today, I know that I'm a good mother at my core. I know, because their father told me so this morning.

Be free with the giving
and receiving of encouragement.

What are human beings that you are mindful of them, . . . ?
Yet you have made them a little lower than God,
and crowned them with glory and honor.
—Psalm 8:4–5

Music

Tonight John walked into the house and turned on some lively music. I wanted to dance and hug and love and even clean up the house, all at the same time—a definite improvement over how I was feeling just prior to his entrance!

I wish I'd think to do that more often during the day. Listening to rousing music could be a mood-lifter for our whole family. It only takes one extra thought, one extra minute, and the returns for the spirit are tenfold. It can turn a tiresome day into one that knows joy!

**Thank you, God,
for the gift of music.**

I will be glad and exult in you;
I will sing praise to your name,
O Most High.

—Psalm 9:2

No Music

This morning I was barely out of bed when John turned on lively music again. He knows I usually have trouble waking up in the morning, and since music worked so well for me yesterday . . .

Well, things can change in twelve hours! Lively music was not what I felt like hearing before breakfast. I thought I was going to crawl out of my skin until I got up enough nerve to tell him I'd rather not receive what he meant as a favor. I couldn't think of a nice way to say it either. The whole episode did give me a clue about why I feel so irritable when I'm awakened by the cries of a child. The sound is too harsh. It wears me out right at the moment when I should be fully rested for another round of parenting!

I long for the morning when I can wake up to quietness and have it continue as long as I want to stay in bed. Now I'm dreaming!

It's okay to dream.
Accept, though,
what is only a dream . . . for now.

For everything there is a season . . .
a time to keep silence,
and a time to speak.

—Ecclesiastes 3:1, 7

Pre-Dinner

I t's one of those necessary evils—having to make dinner at the exact same time my children are hungry and cranky and clinging to my legs, or, worse yet, having another "emergency" in the room farthest from the kitchen. It's the same every night, except for the times their dad works late and we have instant noodle soup.

I could make good dinners. I've done it before. Children's stomachs, however, must be on a different program. I sort of enjoy getting more and more hungry as I smell the onions frying in olive oil and anticipate what will be added to them.

Not so the youngest members of this family! They are playing happily one minute and in the next, they're demanding food in ways that make them seem like totally different people. Pity the parent who doesn't remember history and hasn't at least started dinner.

Often all one can do
in that pre-dinner time of the day
is survive.

Better is a dry morsel with quiet
than a house full of feasting with strife.

—Proverbs 17:1

Sunshine

I don't care how cold it is, we're bundling up and going for a glori-ous walk in the sunshine. Noticing the height of my present spirit, I now realize how continuous days of rain can dampen everything in their path. We've all been more irritable and worn out in spite of sleeping more than usual. This is the first day I've seen the sun all week, and we need to get out and soak in some vitamin D.

Sometimes I need to lose something to bring back my deep appre-ciation for it—like this sunshine. Here's the challenge: to appreciate the sunlight and warmth after we've had it for ten days.

**God, help me nurture
a spirit of gratefulness.**

O send out your light and your truth;
let them lead me;
let them bring me to your holy hill
and to your dwelling.

—Psalm 43:3

Behavior Modification

When I was in school, I remember arguing against behavior modification. I thought children should be allowed to learn their own truths and not be restricted by what an adult decides is the right way. My teacher concluded that session with, "We'll see if your opinion changes when you have children of your own."

Now I do have children and my opinion has had some behavior modification of its own! I still believe children need to be respected as much as possible. I also believe children need to learn limits.

Even if they didn't need limits, I'm discovering my own. I cannot tolerate late bedtimes, a refusal to wash a messy face, or a request for a different meal because someone doesn't like anything on the table, just to name a few. If I'm going to live with these children as long as I hope to, they need to learn my limits as much as I need to honor theirs.

A behavior modification program might be a great place to start. It might be the best way, actually, to make sure the limits are clear to all of us.

Guide me, O God.
I feel an increased need for wisdom.

Give me now wisdom and knowledge
to go out and come in before this people,
for who can rule this great people of yours?

—2 Chronicles 1:10

Anniversaries

Ilove to plan parties. I am energized by preparing to celebrate. But getting ready for Jonathan's birthday this week has left me feeling wiped out and unable to provide him a proper rite of passage into his next year of life.

I finally said my feelings aloud to my husband, who stared at me in disbelief. "You're doing more for this birthday than I've ever seen you do!" he remarked.

His observation reminded me that in the past two years, I was undergoing exploratory surgeries during the week of Jonathan's birthday. Those hospitalizations had consumed my emotional energy.

Now, on the anniversary of those events and fears, I was experiencing emotional uneasiness, which was coinciding with Jonathan's birthday plans. Becoming aware of where my feelings were subconsciously rooted helped me to move on and experience my present good fortune.

Anniversaries of painful events, like an illness or death, often release the original pain again. If I don't acknowledge that, I can stay submerged in sadness and fatigue. Remembering, however, helps me to go on.

**Thank you, God, for heightening my awareness
so that my memories can be healed.**

O Lord my God, I cried to you for help,
and you have healed me.

—Psalm 30:2

Beginning Right

How long is it going to take me to get this into my head? I should not assume, just because it's Saturday, that John has nothing to do but be with the kids while I concentrate on my projects around the house. I shouldn't, but I do. After a busy week, we both need some time alone and we invariably forget that the other person does, too. I forget that I'm not the only worn-out parent here.

So, after each of us was starting in on our own projects and both of us were getting irritated with the children needing our attention (imagine that!), we asked the question we should have begun with this morning, "What are you hoping to do today?"

Opening that channel makes a difference. I hope we learn how to work with each other's needs before the children no longer care about having our attention.

**There's nothing like parenthood
to help me realize how selfish I am.**

Let each of you look not to your own interests,
but to the interests of others.

—Philippians 2:4

Aromatherapy

As I brushed past the overgrown rosemary bush in my garden this morning, its pungent smell invited me to rest a while in its aroma. Of course, someone was yelling for my attention from the house and shattered that moment of living in a poem. I grabbed a sprig to carry with me.

I stuck the rosemary in the buttonhole of my shirt and forgot about it . . . until I knocked against it while reaching for a bowl. It stopped me for a second, for a deep breath of peace. Later, while reading to Maria, her head rested on it and I was filled with a smell that spoke of love. When John came home and it became crushed in the middle of our hug, I took in a breath of joy.

It doesn't take much to remind me of the goodness of life. A simple smell can do it.

Pay attention
to the goodness of smells.

One thing I asked of the LORD, that will I seek after:
to live in the house of the LORD
all the days of my life,
to behold the beauty of the LORD.

—Psalm 27:4

What Were You Saying?

When people ask me what I'm doing with my social work degree, I don't hesitate to acknowledge how much I need and use those trained skills as a parent. There is one skill, however, that I haven't been able to retain lately and that I may be in danger of losing. It's the one about being present with the people talking to me and giving them my undivided attention.

I can't remember the last time I had a complete, uninterrupted conversation. Sometimes after a friend leaves, I think of the many things we talked about and can't remember how they ended. Then I remember: they didn't.

That might be a clue about why I don't see much, anymore, of my friends who don't have children. Those who do still make the effort to stay in touch usually ask if we could get together after the kids are in bed. That's a great solution; only, their bedtime is often my bedtime now, too.

**Believe that your listening skills
are not gone forever.
They are just presently responsible
for more than one thing at a time.**

You must understand this, my beloved:
let everyone be quick to listen, slow to speak,
slow to anger.

—James 1:19

Weekend Company

It's Thursday again, and time to get ready for yet another weekend of guests. When friends called at various times throughout the spring, I happily said we would love for them to come. That wasn't a lie. I am honored that friends want to visit us, and past memories spur me on eagerly to want to create more!

However, this is now our third weekend in a row to entertain out-of-town guests. What I had forgotten was how much work it takes to get ready: planning for and making meals, cleaning, and getting all the weekend projects done ahead of time, or resigning ourselves to having them deleted from the program. It also takes most of Monday to recuperate: washing sheets and towels, cleaning again, and putting things where I like them.

I keep discovering that entertaining is a lot more work now that I have children to care for. Many of our friends bring their children along, which compounds the energy flying around the house.

Friends are certainly a gift. I'm ready to implement some moderation in our entertaining schedule, however, as long as I feel this beat when it's over.

Be thankful that weekends aren't four days!

> May the LORD give strength to his people!
> May the LORD bless his people with peace!
> —Psalm 29:11

Trampled

"I am not your play set!" I hollered as another foot slipped off the top of my head, bent my ear in half, and landed on the shoulder that had been bruised on an earlier climb. My children only giggled and said, "Okay, we'll play sandwich then, and you're the bottom bread!"

They were right to laugh, but it's not always a joke for me. Sometimes I get tired of standing in for a backyard play set. I look for bruises and am surprised if I find none. The children are light-weight, after all, and they don't play with their shoes on.

I'm sure it's healthy for their development to play physically with a parent. Toward the end of a day, though, my body doesn't want any more jolts and stomps, no matter how lightweight!

I'll let their dad help them develop their physical agility. I hereby appoint myself to be the one to help them know limits; they will no longer get out-of-control rough when they play. And those limits take effect immediately, before these kids gain many more pounds.

**God, help me to know
and consistently enforce my limits.**

Be gracious to me, O God,
for people trample on me.

—Psalm 56:1

Faith

"Mommy, I don't want God to be in my heart. Why does God have to be in my heart?" My four-year-old was clearly filled with fear at the thought of anything he couldn't see or understand being inside of him.

Since that day I have fielded questions about God, many of which are hard or impossible to answer. Sometimes the depth of my children's questions leaves me wondering what I understand. Sometimes they help me remember the mystery of God and I join them in their awe. Sometimes they help me see God more simply than the muddle my adult mind creates, and I am again a child, held in God's loving arms.

**Thank you, God, for these children
through whom I experience you.**

Out of the mouths of babes and infants
you have founded a bulwark.

—Psalm 8:2

College or Therapy Fund?

A friend just asked me if we've started college funds for our children. Several responses flew through me simultaneously. First, I've just finished paying off my own college debts! Second, when did paying for college change from being the student's responsibility to the parents'? It was apparently somewhere between when I went and when my children will go. And what if they don't go? A college fund may be a big hopeful assumption on my part. Besides, where will the money for such a fund come from?

Okay, a college fund is not a bad idea. If my children don't go to college, they'll probably need the fund for therapy, to work through the problem of having parents who never saved enough so they could go to college. It's hard to calculate how best to be realistic and fair and supportive.

Guide me, Lord,
in how best to plan
for the future we cannot know.

The human mind plans the way,
but the LORD directs the steps.

—Proverbs 16:9

Safe

I tend to think that these days of weary parenting will be over when I get consistent sleep at night, or when my children can entertain themselves for more than ten minutes at a time. Last night at a party, however, I realized that I may be imagining fantasy.

I was sitting beside a parent of two teenagers. "What really wears me out," she said, "is knowing how old the cars are that we let our girls drive. The later it gets at night, the more I worry until I'm exhausted!"

So much for a good night of sleep any time soon. It looks like once children can sleep through the night, they have other things to do instead! I may be worn out, but at least I know where my children are. They may not sleep all through the night. They may keep me from sleeping all through the night. But they are safe.

**Help me to trust you, God,
now and for my future needs.**

You, O LORD, will protect us.

—Psalm 12:7

Spanking

We have decided not to spank our children. We know that not all parents agree with us. But since we expect our kids to solve their disagreements with words rather than slugs, it makes sense that we should model that for them.

Today it was fortunate I had already made that decision, because I might have hurt my child. I was so angry that my strike would not have been loving discipline. I would have been venting my own violent feelings.

Usually after days like this, when spanking springs to mind as the easiest solution to disobedience, I realize that I have been extremely tired. On these days I am less creative in solving conflicts. I'm less likely to use words. I don't seek guidance from God or friends. These are the days when I need to separate myself from my children long enough to remember how to resolve conflict in a way that leads to peace and deeper love.

**Discipline children on principle,
not on impulse.**

Love is patient.

—1 Corinthians 13:4

Sick Days—Mine

I feel awful. My head's pounding and my whole body is sore and achy. This is a call-in-sick day.

There's only one catch. I'm a mother and I have no one to call. There's no sick leave on this job. If I absolutely couldn't move, I have people who would come and help. This in-between state of just feeling miserable, however, doesn't justify those emergency measures.

So, I'll move slowly and attend only to the essentials of childcare today . . . and pray. That's the best fallback plan a sick mother can generate.

**When you're sick,
take any break you can find.**

Do not be far from me,
for trouble is near and there is no one to help.
—Psalm 22:11

Overwhelmed

I can't even seem to get started on my day! I begin one thing, only to see something else that really should be done first. So I leave the first to do the next, and then discover another, and on, and on. I have myriads of jobs begun; I only wonder when or if I'll finish any of them.

Every room I enter has a mess to clean up. I feel paralyzed with too-much-ness! I can't slow down enough to sort out what's most important from what can wait until another time.

Now that I've realized that much, I'll sit down and think for a minute or three. When I get overwhelmed with tasks, I tend to forget—or be annoyed by—my kids' needs. No wonder they seem to clamor louder than ever on days like this.

Weariness begets weariness.
Break the cycle with some think-time.

All things are wearisome;
more than one can express.

—Ecclesiastes 1:8

Whose Reality?

Last night when John told Maria it was time to pick up her toys, she replied, matter-of-factly, "My royal servants do that for me, Dad." Was she joking, or was she living so deeply within her fantasy that she truly believed her royal lineage exempted her from doing her chores?

It's hard to know, sometimes, when to let children's imaginations possess them, and when to burst their bubbles so they conform to the plans I have for them.

I found Maria funny, but I was also glad to hear what she was thinking. I tend quickly to interpret reluctance to do what I ask as obstinance, needing discipline. More often, it may be that what I perceive as disobedience is simply my child and me not meeting in the same reality.

**Honor the bubbles
from your child's fantasy world.
They will burst soon enough.**

Do not let anything hinder you
from coming to me;
for I will surely do you great honor.

—Numbers 22:16–17

Yes, I'm Tired

When I feel this tired, I imagine that I'm alone in this experience. None of the other parents I see walking around the grocery store or sitting at the park look as worn out as I feel.

I always try to figure out a reason for being tired, as if parenting weren't good enough cause in itself. Today I decided it was the medicine I'm taking. That gave me a bit of satisfaction and I ventured to tell a friend so. I wanted to offer some justification for not helping with the program she's planning.

She just said, "Hmmm, I wonder what my excuse is?" I guess we're all tired from something. Maybe it's not as useful to know why, or to compare myself to others, as to admit it's reality and then accept the limits I need.

**Be as gentle with yourself
as you would be with a good friend.**

Guard me as the apple of the eye;
hide me in the shadow of your wings.

—Psalm 17:8

Speak Encouragement

When I was young, I liked listening to my parents talking to their friends. I especially loved it when I heard them tell someone how well I was doing in school or about the good muffins I baked for dinner that week or about a special project I was creating. I don't remember ever hearing them say anything bad to their friends about me.

I'm thankful for that memory currently, when I find myself sharing my frustrations about my children with my friends. When they were infants it didn't matter. Now, even when the children are busily engaged, they are likely listening to my conversation if they are anywhere within earshot. I can either embarrass them or let them know how proud I am of them, depending upon what I say when they can hear.

**Lord, help me share
in my children's hearing
only the things
that will build them up in love.**

Glorious things are spoken of you.

—Psalm 87:3

Plans

Why do I even bother making plans? At the beginning of the week, I religiously make a list of what I need or want to do in the days ahead. I don't want to forget anything, and I also get a sense of accomplishment whenever I cross things off the list.

Almost as if they planned it, my children have a way of messing up my best efforts at a schedule. Today my daughter woke up with a fever, which threw off every plan I had. We won't go out, no one will come here, and I must remember that she will need some extra love and patience.

The change-up is not always as drastic as a fever, but rarely do my children consult my list before they get grumpy or make messes or demand that I play with them. I'm the one in control here, right? Well, maybe! Maybe one job children have is to help me remember that few things carry the importance I assign to them.

If you have to live by lists,
put "Love my children"
at the top.

Change your mind
and do not bring disaster on your people.
—Exodus 32:12

Getting Out the Door

I can't believe I still haven't gotten this timing down. After ten years, I still expect that when I say, "Let's go," we will go. Silly me. I'm even gracious enough to give little warnings sometimes. I say, "We have to go in ten minutes." But in ten minutes, the children are no closer to being ready than if I hadn't spoken. Then I get impatient at the very time I want harmony—and I hate remembering all day what a nag I was getting them out of the house. I wonder if they remember it all day, too, and I pray they don't.

I vow to do better the next time. I'll start to leave earlier. I'll help them get their sweaters on. I'll have all my stuff done so I can stand right beside them and keep them focused on preparing to leave.

Either way, it's wearing. Getting out of the house on time can be one of the great hurdles of the day.

**Lord, forgive me for the times
I think my children
are the only ones
who have a hard time focusing.**

By paths they have not known

I will guide them.

—Isaiah 42:16

The Pain of a Friend

One of my friends just found out that she has breast cancer. She's my age and has young children, too. I'm torn suddenly with many emotions: shock, grief for her and her family, an eagerness to do something for her—cook, babysit, send flowers, write a card (it all seems inadequate). And fear. I'm afraid to see her. What should I say? I'm afraid for myself. If it's happened to her, it could just as easily happen to me.

I want to see her and I don't. I want to offer her my love and I want to run the other direction. I want to be available to her, whatever that means. But I can feel my life energy draining from me just thinking about what she must be going through. I'm consumed with her pain and, indirectly, my own.

**When paralyzed with grief or fear,
prayer is usually a good place to start.**

The Spirit helps us in our weakness;
for we do not know how to pray as we ought,
but that very Spirit intercedes
with sighs too deep for words.

—Romans 8:26

Gratefulness

I've been walking around today thinking about how wonderful it is that I don't have cancer! I'm not feeling smug because my friend does, but I'm immensely grateful for my health, which I usually take for granted. My friend's crisis is making me more aware of what a gift life is.

I'm looking at my children as if this were my last year with them. What all would I want to do with them and for them? What words do I want to leave for them in a journal?

I'm seeing the beauty of my home instead of all the improvements that I'd like to make. I'm noticing all the friends who weave in and out of my life. I'm feeling thankful for the endless love and support I receive from my husband. Life seems very rich and full right now.

**Don't wait for bad news
to appreciate life.**

I will give thanks to the Lord
with my whole heart.

—Psalm 9:1

Misunderstandings

I heard a wail coming from the bathroom. "Mommy, there's a bug in the bathtub!"

Heroically, I swooped in, grabbed a tissue, and crushed that little ant before it could go another step closer to my daughter.

But the wail intensified tenfold, leaving me baffled. "But I didn't want you to kill it!" she yelled.

Where was this new attitude coming from? "My Sunday School teacher said God made all the animals," she continued, "so we shouldn't kill them."

"So," I wondered aloud, "why did you yell for me to come get it?"

"I just wanted you to take it outside."

Now how was I supposed to know that? My logical conclusions are not always child-sensible. I'll try to remember that in the face of future "emergencies."

**Parents must accept this fact:
our best is not always
our children's desire.**

Give ear to my words, O Lord;
give heed to my sighing.

—Psalm 5:1

Honoring Parenthood

At Maria's eighth birthday party, the mother of one of her guests showed up with a gift for me! She said that after being a parent for eight years, I deserved a gift as much as Maria did. It was a book on what to expect from my eight-year-old.

I was flabbergasted by her sensitivity and generosity. I had never thought of celebrating children's birthdays with a gift to the parents. It makes a lot of sense. I did deserve to mark the anniversary of birthing this child, for my own growth as well as hers. The book was a wonderful boost to my parenting. My years at this job were honored in that moment and every time I've remembered the gift since then.

This is an idea I want to pass on to other parents on the birthdays of their children.

**Make plans to honor
a friend's parenting.**

Out of them shall come thanksgiving,
and the sound of merrymakers.
I will make them many, and they shall not be few;
I will make them honored.

—Jeremiah 30:19

Spontaneity

Last year after spending an evening decorating our Christmas tree, none of us wanted to leave the magic of the lights and decorations to go to our separate bedrooms. So, instead, each of us got our pillow and blankets and found a spot on the living room floor. We snuggled in for bedtime stories and fell asleep listening to Christmas music.

This year when my children's teachers asked them to share the special traditions their family has at Christmas, they both said that our whole family always sleeps under the tree the night we decorate it! Tradition doesn't have to take a long time to develop. It can happen by acting on one spontaneous idea.

**Surprise your children
with an act of spontaneity!**

The boundary lines have fallen for me
in pleasant places;
I have a goodly heritage.

—Psalm 16:6

Building Self-Confidence

Sleeping under the Christmas tree reminds me of another spontaneous act which has not become a tradition, but is a great memory. It was a rainy summer day, and my daughter wanted to play out her ideas in the kitchen.

She pulled everything from the refrigerator and snack cupboard that didn't have to be cooked and asked for bowls to fill. She then announced that we were going to have a picnic. The rain apparently hadn't registered with her.

In one grace-filled moment of inspiration, I suggested we have the picnic on our living room floor. I quickly pulled out a bright yellow tablecloth and we set the "table" with her picnic choices. It didn't matter what dinner consisted of that night. I was too tired to think of anything else, and she was delighted to have engineered the event.

**It's never too early
to build a child's self-confidence.**

My heart is glad, and my soul rejoices;
my body also rests secure.

—Psalm 16:9

When Parents Disagree

Tonight I'm grateful for the many times my husband and I agree on how to raise our children, because it sure is hard when we don't. It takes enough energy to withstand the kids' complaints when he and I do agree.

When I don't really care if they eat more candy at the party like all their friends are doing, but Dad has already said, "No," that's when I hardly have the energy to deal! I think they know I'm the soft one on this issue, too, because I'm the one they keep asking.

Considering the broader picture, I know it's important for parents to provide a united front. It's less confusing to children, even if they don't like it. But when our parental impulses are different, developing a joint policy is a lot of work.

**Putting energy in the right places now
will save energy later.**

You anoint my head with oil;
my cup overflows.

—Psalm 23:5

Single Parenting

The epitome of exhaustion for me is waking up in my son's bed and discovering that my daughter's light is still on. She's reading in her room because no one has tucked her in yet.

My friend, whose husband left her two years ago, stated it matter-of-factly, but I heard in her words a depth of sorrow where she couldn't afford to let herself live. She's the only parent in the house, so whatever doesn't get done is her omission. Decisions are hers alone to make. Caring for her children has to happen with whatever energy only she has available. No one is coming home to relieve or accompany her.

Pray for a single parent.

O God, do not be far from me;
O my God, make haste to help me!

—Psalm 71:12

Accidents

One minute I was laughing with my son as I pushed him on the park swing, and the next minute he was on the ground screaming. Blood gushed from his head, and self-accusation came just as fast at me.

How could I have let him fall, standing right behind him? How could I have missed seeing that rock directly under the swing? Why did I think he was old enough to hang on by himself?

Holding him to my chest, all I could say was, "I'm sorry. I'm so sorry, Jonathan." Someone else stopped the bleeding. Someone else cleaned the blood off both of us. Someone else absolved my guilt with a simple, "It wasn't your fault."

It's a wonder any child ever makes it to adulthood! It's no wonder parents raise kids, exhausted!

**Pray each day
for the grace to handle
the unexpected
that will surely come.**

Surely, God is my helper;
the LORD is the upholder of my life.

—Psalm 54:4

Blessed Present

Sometimes I look at photos of my children at a younger age and wish that we were still in that stage. I loved their tiny hands, grasping my fingers with total love and trust. I miss the wide eyes that told me I was all they needed. Falling asleep with arms entangled was to know ecstasy.

Sometimes I watch a mother having dinner at a restaurant with her teenage daughter and my heart grows tender, eager to have that kind of a relationship. I want to talk about feelings together and hear my child solve the problems of the world.

Today, though, I don't have the past or the future. I have the present, which is a true gift when I live aware of its own possibilities.

**God, help me bless
the present.**

If we hope for what we do not see,
we wait for it with patience.

—Romans 8:25

Lighten Up!

A woman asked a group of us today if we had any advice about giving allowances to children.

The first woman was adamant that her way was the best. Ever since her children were six years old, she has given them as many dollars each week as the years they have lived. They are then responsible for buying everything they want.

Another woman said her children earn their allowance by doing chores. She conceded that she hasn't paid them for months because her kids would rather not work.

I jumped in, saying that I think chores should be done because each person is a part of the family, and that allowances should not be connected to how much one cooperates.

Others offered variations and additional opinions. I was left feeling like I had been in a washing machine, twisted back and forth, trying to figure out the best, cleanest way to do allowances.

Some issues are not clearly cut between right and wrong. The more we weigh the various options, the more wearisome it becomes.

**When making decisions,
review the evidence to your satisfaction,
trust your gut, and get on with life.**

What do people gain from all the toil
at which they toil under the sun?

—Ecclesiastes 1:3

Death

If it were up to me, I would not have chosen this time for my grandma to die. Life is really unfair, all the way to the end.

My children are just old enough to have bonded with her, but not old enough to deal with death. At least I wish they wouldn't have to yet. But then I wish I wouldn't have to yet either.

I want to go off with my parents and siblings and cry by ourselves. But I have children now, who have to find something to do with their own feelings, and I can't leave them.

I don't grieve alone anymore. Sometimes that's comforting. Today it takes more energy than I think I have to give.

**Lord, give me
an extra measure of
patience and wisdom.**

Precious in the sight of the Lord
is the death of his faithful ones.

—Psalm 116:15

Grief

It's odd. The whole weekend of my grandma's funeral, with its accompanying activities, played out completely differently than I had expected and feared.

Instead of my kids being an extra bother and emotional drain, I found I needed them probably more than they needed me. I found myself talking about why Grandma died, although I didn't know I needed to explore that until they asked. I needed to talk about how she had lived and why I loved her so much. They wanted to hear my stories. I needed to hug and be hugged. They acquiesced.

They wanted to know where Grandma went. I felt my attitude change from sorrow to deep inner peace when I heard myself tell them she's happy now, living with God. I was glad for that reminder. I was also glad for their response of celebration, "Then we'll see her again!" and "You mean she's not sick anymore?"

God, thank you for the gift of being bonded to the faith of my children.

The Lord protects the simple;
when I was brought low, he saved me.

—Psalm 116:6

Tears

My children saw me cry last night for the first time. I was aware that seeing my tears was new for them and that they probably didn't understand what was happening. But I was so sad and hurt that I couldn't stop.

I didn't want to stop actually. I believe in the goodness and healing power of crying and I wanted to model that.

I know that it can be scary for children to see their parents cry and that they sometimes feel responsible for the tears. They were unexpectedly sharing my sadness; I did not also want them to be scared or feel responsible for the tears. When I could talk again, I asked them how they felt about me crying. They said it didn't bother them.

Maybe it didn't. Maybe it did and they didn't want to talk about it. To be safe, I assured them that I was crying because I was sad and it wasn't their fault.

Now I have to trust their ability to accept it. I'll see if I can do that.

**Living life together,
especially the parts that are uncomfortable,
makes it more tolerable.**

I have been a sanctuary to them for a little while.
—Ezekiel 11:16

More on Crying

After I so boldly defended tears and stated my belief that healing can come through them, I must also say that a part of me doesn't want my children to see me cry. I want to hide my vulnerabilities from them. I want them to think of me only as a strong mother who has everything under control. I want to protect them from hurt: mine, theirs, and the world's.

That's not reality, though. Pain is part of life.

Even if I could act like nothing hurts me, how would that serve my children? How can they accept that pain will come to them if they don't see me accepting it? How can they live with hurt and know that it can be endured if they haven't watched how I handle being hurt?

I don't like feeling weak or being hurt. I can only fully experience my strength, however, after I know what it's like to be vulnerable. I want my children to learn how real strength is built. So I guess they'll see more of my tears.

Thank you, God,
for meeting me where I am,
in strength and in tears.

Hear my cry, O God;
listen to my prayer.

—Psalm 61:1

Meltdown

Yesterday, at the end of a wonderful weekend together at a mountain resort, our family stopped at a quaint little gift shop, one of those with quaint big prices attached to everything. When my daughter asked if she could buy something, I said I'd be glad to buy her a postcard to remember the weekend. She wanted a stuffed animal.

I saw no reason for a discussion. We had just spent a little bundle of money on an extravagant weekend, and I know how many stuffed animals she already sleeps with. Besides, I've watched this drama over and over: the toy so desperately needed for happiness lies unnoticed forevermore after the first week of passion. My answer was clearly, "No."

She cried and wailed and accused me of being unfair all the way down the mountain. My anger was rising quickly and I began to argue with her, when my husband mouthed to me, "She's really tired."

Sure enough, two minutes later she had cried herself to sleep in the backseat. I relaxed in the front. She never brought it up again.

Children, too, get tired.

As God's chosen ones,
holy and beloved,
clothe yourselves with compassion,
kindness, humility, meekness, and patience.

—Colossians 3:12

Just Say No

When our family returned from our three-day weekend in the mountains last night, there were fourteen messages on our answering machine. A couple were already outdated, but half were requests for my time and three-quarters of them required a return call.

Nothing can quite cut the effect of refreshing mountain air like the call of responsibility. Any relaxation I had accumulated vanished in those minutes after I pressed the replay button. I felt paralyzed, not able, even, to unpack.

I finally decided that the world had gone on without my normal presence for three days, and I would pretend I was on vacation one more night. I could immediately breathe more easily and was able to begin putting things away.

This morning I was ready to be here again. That's probably because I decided last night to say no to the rest of the world.

**Thank you, God,
for helping me understand
what I needed.**

Be still before the LORD,
and wait patiently for him.

—Psalm 37:7

Meals

Mealtime can be magical. It's a reminder that we're living in a holy moment. We have a chance as a family to gather together for nourishment, physically and emotionally, after our involvement in different activities all day.

So why is it so hard to keep holiness in those moments? Why do I spend so much time saying, "Don't eat with your fingers," or, "Sit back down, please."? Why am I tempted to give the kids a couple of heavy snacks or let them eat in front of the television on the nights John doesn't come home for dinner? Why, when he is home, do we find it easier to talk about adult stuff, leaving the children out of the conversation?

Many times I need to act upon the decision I've already made, that we will sit down together for meals whenever possible. If I act, instead, on my feelings of the moment, my children may never know my values. I might never find out what has happened in their minds and in their worlds that day. I might miss some moments of holiness.

**Be prepared for some holiness
at your next meal.**

My child, give me your heart,
and let your eyes observe my ways.

—Proverbs 23:26

Love Languages

I'm fascinated by the idea that people respond to different love languages, to certain ways they hear love best. Some people know they are loved by words, when another says, "I love you." Others aren't moved by talking as much as if someone does something useful for them, like making dinner or fixing the washing machine. Some feel love when they are physically touched; some like to be given gifts.

As luck of human nature would have it, my love language is different than my husband's. It takes a lot of work to remember to love him with his language rather than my own, which I do more naturally.

I don't know yet what my children's love languages are. Maybe they are able to soak up love by whatever mode it comes. The best tactic is to love them with as many languages as possible until I figure out which one they are understanding most clearly.

Try to love your child
in each love language today:
touching, talking, doing something for her,
giving a small gift.

You shall love the Lord your God with all your heart,
and with all your soul,
and with all your mind.

—Matthew 22:37

Body Check

At any given moment of the day, if I pay attention to my body, I'm tensing up some part of it. It's either my shoulders or my stomach, my back or my neck. Sometimes they're all tight, like I'm getting ready for a whistle to start the race. Even when I'm sitting down and think I'm relaxed, if I become conscious of where I'm holding tension, I can usually relax my body another notch or two.

Years ago, a friend told me that it's a good practice to observe my body at least once every hour. If I ask it how it's feeling, and then relieve it of any stress it doesn't need to be carrying, I'll be healthier in general.

That was good advice. I wish I could remember to do it more often. Maybe then my back and neck wouldn't be persistently tired.

God, help me to be attentive
to what my body is telling me.

Glorify God in your body.

—1 Corinthians 6:20

Too Tired to Sleep

I hate it when my body is exhausted but my mind is too busy to let me sleep. I begin longing for that prone position by late afternoon, but when I finally hit the pillow, I can't get my head to stop racing. Whenever I have a lot going on I have this compulsion to plan the rest of my week over and over, I guess to make sure it all still fits together. I don't know why I do it, and I haven't learned to control the urge.

I should at least be able to stop thinking about what I'm going to wear when I get up. If I could just go to sleep, I'd have time to consider that in the morning. Unless I am willful about putting all such little details to rest, however, they pop up, uninvited and powerful! And if I give any thought at all to the fact that staying awake is really frustrating me, I'm more awake than ever.

Sometimes it helps if I have a word or phrase to repeat over and over, to replace the repetitive plans that otherwise persist. "All is well" or "I'm so tired" have worked for me.

**Find a word or phrase that calms you
when you have too many thoughts to sleep.**

With your faithful help
rescue me from sinking in the mire.

—Psalm 69:13–14

Waiting

I waited all day for the phone to ring. I called my doctor's office early this morning to find out the results of yesterday's test. The nurse said she would have the doctor call me back.

I should have asked when she thought that might be, but I didn't want to sound too pushy. Now I wish I had asked because I've stayed home all day, waiting. I didn't make any of the phone calls I thought of throughout the day because I didn't want to tie up the line. When friends called, I said I'd have to call them back later. I was waiting for an important call.

I find myself still waiting, long after I'm sure the office is closed. My nervous anticipation of the day has turned to anger. Now I'm too tired to make the personal calls I've put off all day.

Waiting patiently is a virtue, I'm sure. I'm also sure it's a virtue I don't have. Waiting wears me out!

**Help me know when I need to wait
and when I need to get back on the phone
and push.**

Lead me in your truth, and teach me,
for you are the God of my salvation;
for you I wait all day long.

—Psalm 25:5

Post-Crisis

This is the day when I should be dancing and shouting for joy. My friends are calling to say how happy they are that the test results came back negative—which is positive for me! They wonder what I'm doing to celebrate. For them, the crisis is over.

For me, this is the day when I can start taking deep breaths again and begin to realize how much energy has been drained from my body and soul. I can finally give myself permission to feel my emotions. I can stop being responsible for holding myself together. Now I can cry.

This part I will do alone because my friends were glad for good news and have moved on. They are not insensitive. They simply don't know, unless I put out a little more energy to explain why it's not yet all over for me.

God, help me remember
this post-crisis loneliness,
so that I can walk beside
my friends in the future
who will travel this path.

Save me, O God,
for the waters have come up to my neck.

—Psalm 69:1

Gratefully Angry

Is it possible to be grateful and angry at the same time? It must be, because I'm feeling both today.

I'm grateful that the doctor's report has declared me healthy. Now that the blood work, X-rays, and the waiting to hear the results are over, and now that I can get back to my normal routine, I have time to realize how maddening the whole process has been. Extra appointments, to which I can't take my children, are something no parent has time for. This whole episode has taken two weeks out of my time emotionally. It has required worry energy that I can't seem to refuse giving when a doctor says, "Hmm, we better check this out."

Now that it's over, I don't want to give it another minute of my time or energy. But maybe if I can admit that I'm angry, I will recover faster. I also remind myself that anger doesn't negate my gratefulness. I can carry both.

**God, thank you
for accepting and understanding
the strange emotional combinations
I hold within me.**

Trust in him at all times, O people;
pour out your heart before him;
God is a refuge for us.

—Psalm 62:8

Instructive Dreams

I've never practiced recording my dreams, but I don't want to lose the one I woke up remembering this morning. I want to keep the mood of it, at least as long as I can.

I was in my own home. My husband and children all looked the same, but we were all older. We were having dinner and laughing about the events of the day.

It was not spectacular. Instead, it was the ordinary yet amazing peacefulness of being together that sticks with me. The dream felt like a promise of years to come; that in spite of our current stress, we will be well. The support we gain from each other will continue to give each of us strength and joy to grow.

> **Dreams can be another avenue**
> **God uses to communicate with me.**

I bless the LORD who gives me counsel;
in the night also my heart instructs me.

—Psalm 16:7

Night Terrors

Jonathan called me to his room at 1:00 this morning, terrified by the dream he was having.

A wild animal was coming toward him, and then he saw that it was getting me. He didn't want to go back to sleep. He was afraid the animal would still be there.

Even though half asleep, I figured out what was happening. Jonathan doesn't have a way, yet, to articulate all his fears when he's awake. He's felt the recent stress in our family, however, and his dreams are helping him deal with it.

When I'm under stress, I try to keep things as normal as possible for my children. I forget that any sensitive child, no matter how young, will feel the underlying tension. Maybe if I would acknowledge our family fears with him, at a level he can understand, they wouldn't turn into monsters he has to conquer at night. When he is pursued by them, however, I will continue to let him know that he is safe.

**Help me, Lord,
to know that my job
is not to keep all fear and bad things
away from my children,
but to let them know they are safe with me.**

You alone, O Lord,
make me lie down in safety.

—Psalm 4:8

Necessary Shoulds

I don't want to sit in the hospital with my friend tomorrow while her husband is in surgery. I don't like hospitals. I get tense just walking into one. I don't like to wait either. I feel so helpless, like I'm part of an out-of-control nothingness.

Apparently, no one else wants to sit with her either. I waited until yesterday to ask if she had someone to be with her. I assumed that somebody was already lined up, but that I would appear to be willing. Well, my offer was the first she got.

I usually try not to do things just because I should. This, however, is a sisterly should; one I need to do because this woman is part of my community. No one else is filling this gap. Maybe no one else thought of it. It seems to be mine to do.

**God, give me the strength to fulfill
this "should."**

This I know, that God is for me.

—Psalm 56:9

Stress Overload

After I resigned myself to spending all the time necessary waiting at the hospital with my friend, I did it more willingly. After I got there and we started visiting, the compelling "should" I had felt, gave way to wanting to help her through the wait.

I was doing well, anyway, until I locked my keys in the car after a quick stop to pick up the kids on the way home. My spare key, money, and bank card lay right there on the front seat looking at me.

Locking keys in the car is a sure sign that I'm on stress overload. Today in the hospital, less than a week after my own hospital tests, was too much.

I'm still glad I did what I thought I should. Sometimes, however, I'm just glad to have made it through the day, no matter how much the locksmith charges.

**Lord, whether or not I walked the best path today,
thank you for being there with me
and for caring.**

You have kept count of my tossings;
put my tears in your bottle.

—Psalm 56:8

Dinner Delivered

When I got home from doing ten million errands yesterday, I found a bag on my doorstep. In it were a bag of muffins, two containers of chili that were still warm, and a bowl of rice with instructions for how long to bake it.

I was stunned! Sure, I'm having a rough week, and, true, I didn't have a clue about what we were having for dinner, but this meal was completely unexpected. What a gift! Immediate relief surged into my every pore—the kind I usually don't let in while there are still things to do.

Later, when I found out who had prepared and delivered my delightful surprise, Crystal quickly assured me that she didn't expect me to return the favor. She said she only does this kind of thing when she wants to.

All I know is that last night I was extremely thankful that she listened to her heart. It opened my heart, too, to the possibility of someday hearing similar instructions.

It is comforting to have a friend
who listens to her heart.
I want to be one of those kinds of friends.

In everything do to others
as you would have them do to you.

—Matthew 7:12

Mess or Creativity?

My daughter has discovered the joy of food coloring. She adds drops of yellow and green and red to little jars of water, then labels them "sunshine" and "cactus juice" and "crushed rose petals." She turns vanilla pudding into a beautiful sunset with swirls of yellow and red. This is the romantic version.

In this afternoon's version she used up the whole bottle of red coloring, stained the counter with the blue, and walked away from her creations to the next activity, leaving a total kitchen disaster in her wake. I was ready to banish her from my cooking ingredients forever, in a not-so-kind sort of way.

Luckily for her, John walked in at that exact moment and told me that someday, when she becomes a famous chef, she will give me all the credit and thank me for allowing her to experiment in our kitchen.

She still had to clean up her mess. My frustrated accusations, however, had been turned into a desire to teach responsibility. I needed that alternative observation.

**Attempt to recognize the creativity
beneath the mess.**

He reached down from on high,
he took me;
he drew me out of mighty waters.

—Psalm 18:16

Teaching Forgiveness

"I'm sorry for yelling so much tonight," I confessed as I tucked my child into bed. "I was angry that you weren't listening to me, but I wish I wouldn't have yelled at you. Will you forgive me?"

My child quickly granted forgiveness. He also apologized for his part in the rough evening both of us had.

Some experts on child-rearing say parents should never apologize to their children. That makes no sense to me, though, unless they never do anything wrong. (I think I'd like to meet that parent.) How else will children learn to admit failure themselves, if they don't hear their parents admit failure? How else will they learn to apologize when they do wrong? How else will they learn to grant forgiveness?

Apologies are not fun. My behavior that leads to my need to apologize is almost unbearable. But when I receive forgiving love from my child, my soul finds healing. I move one step further away from continuing that behavior.

**Thank you, Lord, for giving our family
ways to heal the hurts we cause each other.**

And forgive us our sins,
for we ourselves forgive everyone indebted to us.
—Luke 11:4

Faith

Savor the Day

On good days, I want my children to stay at their present stages forever. Each new phase is my favorite so far. The more they can communicate and reason and know, the closer I feel to them.

On bad days, I act like all I want is for my kids to hurry up and grow up. In my frustration, I actually said to them recently, "You are acting so childish!"

Did they hear the irony in that, like I did as soon as it was out of my mouth? I hope they forget I said it.

God, help me to enjoy each stage
and to live in the knowledge
that I will never retrieve these moments.

Jesus said, "Let the little children come to me,
and do not stop them;
for it is to such as these
that the kingdom of heaven belongs."
—Matthew 19:14

Easy Living

I've been thinking about all those parents of past generations, and all those people who live with few or no conveniences, and how much effort they put into living. Then I think about my life and how much work I think it is. That led me to consider my vacuum cleaner, washer, dryer, and dishwasher. I have a stove, oven, food processor, microwave, electric skillet, wok, Hot Shot, and two coffeemakers. I turn on any of seven spigots in the house and water comes out. I flip switches and light finds whatever corner I want. I turn knobs to warm or cool our home.

If I'm this busy and this tired with all of these conveniences, how did my grandma ever do it? She made her own pie crusts, too, and sewed her own clothes, while raising six children.

In many ways, I live in circumstances where it's never been easier to survive. I'm glad to be living here and now, even if it does take a lot of energy to run all my machines!

**Go on a camping trip to regain
a good perspective on the ease of living.**

It is God's gift that all should eat and drink
and take pleasure in all their toil.

—Ecclesiastes 3:13

Miscarriage Memories

At the playground today, I found myself watching the children who looked like they were about eight years old. That's how old our first child would be this month if I hadn't had the miscarriage.

I watched the boys and wondered if I had been pregnant with a son. Would he have had blonde hair like the boy running past me? Would he love to ride a bike and rollerblade?

I watched the girls, too, and imagined what my eight-year-old daughter would be like. Maybe she would be at a sassy stage like the girl telling her mother she wasn't ready to go home yet. Of all the sizes and shapes I could see, which would she most closely embody?

With the passing of years and the gift of more children, the pain of that first loss decreases. I don't suppose, though, that I will ever forget.

Respect the added weariness
that memories provide.

These things I remember,
as I pour out my soul.

—Psalm 42:4

Baby Weight?

Well, I guess I can no longer blame this weight on having a baby. When my youngest is old enough to ask, "Mommy, do you have another baby in there?" it's a pretty big hint that this stomach is not shrinking without a little more help from me.

I know what the trouble is. I eat when I'm tired. I eat to comfort my sadness. I calm myself with food. I sleep better when I have a little something at bedtime (or so I tell myself). I eat because it's fun. I clean up the children's plates so the food doesn't go to waste.

I'm ready to lose some of this weight. I don't know about changing my food habits though. That's a lot of work!

Those women who shrink back to their former size when their baby is a month old make me tired. Maybe I don't want to badly enough.

**Don't waste energy wishing
for what you're not ready to do.**

Do not worry about your life, what you will eat,
or about your body, what you will wear.
For life is more than food,
and the body more than clothing.

—Luke 12:22–23

Repeated Training

I get so tired of picking up after my children—their clothes, their toys, their dirt. I know they're old enough to be doing it themselves, and usually I make them, but that takes energy in itself. When I'm too tired, it's easier to do it myself, and that makes me angry.

I was complaining about this to my mother, thinking she could give me some tips about how she got my siblings and me to be tidy. Instead, she told me, "Oh, don't worry. They'll pick up after themselves by the time they leave home."

I hope she was kidding. Her reply did help me to lower my expectations a little and to see this learning process as a small piece of a bigger life. My kids probably will pick up after themselves eventually, but only if I keep teaching them to be responsible.

Be sure you see the full picture
of growing up.

Train children in the right way,
and when old, they will not stray.

—Proverbs 22:6

Unique Personalities

Is it arrogant or unfair of me to ask my children to meet my standards of orderliness? Should I try to instill in them that the right way to keep house is having each thing in place, just because I like it that way? Maybe my children won't think keeping a neat house is important, no matter how energetically I try to teach them that it is.

My children's personalities have some overlap with mine, but they also have unique aspects that I may never understand. For them to grow confident in who they are, I need to respect them.

Different views about how to keep house are not moral issues. I don't have to insist that this be on my already lengthy list of things that wear me out.

**Decide what issues are worth
using your precious energy
resources to enforce.**

He blesses
the abode of the righteous.

—Proverbs 3:33

Violence

I can't clear my head of the picture from this morning's newspaper. I couldn't bear to read the whole story about the infant found dead in the microwave, but the haunting image lingers inside of me.

I'm remembering a similar event that happened in my dreams, years ago when I was pregnant. I dreamed that I put my baby in the oven to keep it warm. At the time, I assumed my dreams were helping me deal with the uncertainties of my impending parenthood. I wondered what realities the parents of today's newspaper baby were dealing with.

It's easy to condemn such atrocities. Calling them atrocities, in itself, puts distance between the ones who committed them and myself. It's much harder to look at my own capacity to make wrong choices and to inflict damage on another. Unless I'm willing to face myself, however, the energy it takes to be a false, self-avowed saint will absolutely exhaust me! Then I really could hurt someone.

**Lord, help me admit my own capacity
to commit violent acts and think violent thoughts
and to bring them under your control.**

Protect me, O God, for in you I take refuge.
I say to the Lord,
"You are my Lord; I have no good apart from you."
—Psalm 16:1–2

Tired Spouse

Dinner was over in a fraction of the time it had taken me to prepare it. Nothing unusual there. I sat alone at the table, staring blankly at all the leftover food and dirty dishes, wondering where I could get the energy to clean it up. Then I heard something unusual.

I walked toward the noise and found my husband lying in front of the television. My stare was no longer blank; it was full of darts.

"What's wrong?" he asked.

"You could have at least cleared your own dish!"

"I was going to help. I just needed a short break first."

My streak of anger passed. He was tired, too. We had both worked hard all week. I suddenly remembered the previous day when he was busy sorting through a pile of papers in the den while I fell asleep in the living room. He hadn't punished me. I hurried to clean up the dinner table, remembering that he, too, deserved to rest.

**Happiness depends on refusing to keep records
of who does the most household chores.**

Let my beloved come to his garden,
and eat its choicest fruits.
—Song of Solomon 4:16

Perspective

Usually when I return from being gone all weekend, I'm worn a little thin. I don't feel like unpacking. I want another whole day to settle in at home before I have to jump into my routine again.

This time I'm tired, but not in the same pooped way. I have just spent a weekend with women who are divorced, some of whom are remarried, many of whom are working at blending families.

As I remember their stories and their struggle to make life bearable, I realize that there are many forms of weariness I haven't had to learn. I don't minimize my own pain or exhaustion next to theirs, but they have given me a new perspective.

No matter how hard my life is, I would still rather have my life than anyone else's. No matter how tired I am, I know people who have many more pieces to juggle than I do. Yes, I'm tired going into this next week. But I'm carrying a grateful fatigue, one I can live with.

**Hearing the weariness of others' struggles
puts mine in perspective.**

My God will fully satisfy every need of yours
according to his riches in glory in Christ Jesus.
—Philippians 4:19

Divorced

One of the women I met on my weekend retreat was recently divorced. She thought the divorce would solve a lot of her problems, but admits it has created many others. She no longer has to put up with her husband yelling at her or otherwise keeping her from doing what she wants to do. The fact that they have children together, however, has only made their communication problems grow more complex. Now they have to decide where the children will be and when. They not only need to taxi the children to activities and friends, but also back and forth between their homes. They must agree on where their children will go to school and when they are available to go on each of their vacations.

Choosing to get away from her husband has meant that she is also away from her children more of the time. They will be forever split during major holidays and events. She has given up more than a husband. She is also grieving the loss of part of her children's lives.

Lord have mercy.
Christ have mercy.
Grant us peace.

Evening and morning and at noon
I utter my complaint and moan,
and he will hear my voice.

—Psalm 55:17

Double Exhaustion

I am learning that divorce has at least as many faces as marriage. While some former spouses maintain amiable relations with their children's other parent, many others are embroiled in vicious battles for custody. The financial and emotional stress that all these separations put on both parents and children is huge.

Some children have to tell a judge which parent they want to live with. Many are court-ordered to spend time with each parent, whether or not they're comfortable with both. That can mean packing suitcases to move twice a week or more, and packing up the emotions that fly between homes, as well.

Parents who are divorced no longer have only their own weariness to live with. They find themselves helping their children learn about an adult kind of exhaustion.

Letting children talk about hard feelings
as early as possible
will help them know they are safe.

My heart is in anguish within me . . .
Fear and trembling come upon me,
and horror overwhelms me.

—Psalm 55:4–5

Remarriage

I talked with a woman caught in the ups and downs of possibly remarrying. She was divorced when her children were young. They don't remember ever living with their father, and he rarely visits them. Despite that, the children have, during the past seven years, fantasized about their perfect family. Their biological parents were going to someday fall in love again and remarry, just like in the movies.

Now full of joy about her plans to marry another man, this woman is faced with her children's disappointment over their foiled fantasy family. They don't want someone new to enter the only family they have ever known or dreamed about.

I remember how much work it was to plan my wedding. It must be wearing beyond comprehension to plan a wedding and life beyond, while also caring for children who resist it.

**Life is a juggle of
joy and grief.**

O that I had wings like a dove!
I would fly away and be at rest.

—Psalm 55:6

Blended Families

Anya was happy beyond belief after remarrying; her husband had died suddenly four years before. She was elated to be a complete family again, for herself and her two girls.

Her joy was quickly tempered, however, by the tension of relating to her new husband's daughter. The daughter visited on holidays and every other weekend. Anya was trying to give her all the love and assurance she could, to make her feel welcome in her dad's new family.

Anya's own children resented their mother's attention being split with a girl who wasn't their sister. Her husband's daughter, at the same time, disliked that two other girls were living with her father.

It's all understandable jealousy. It's all a groping for love. It's all very depleting of life energy. Many of us are living with its reality.

**Give yourself credit
for the juggling act you are living.**

You will have confidence,
because there is hope;
you will be protected
and take your rest in safety.

—Job 11:18

Date Your Spouse

When our firstborn daughters came to us several weeks apart, Julie and I became friends. We got the children together to play. We supported each other through the hard stages and celebrated the fun ones. By the time the girls were out of diapers, they each had a baby brother.

With two children each, Julie and I both felt an increased need to have time alone with our husbands. And we each had decreased resources to pay for childcare. We began swapping children once a month to give the other couple a date night.

Having a date with John once every other month didn't seem like much, but had we not consistently planned for it always a month in advance, it wouldn't have happened even that often!

Seven years later, we are still swapping. Our children are great friends and our marriages have been enriched many times over.

Plan a date with your spouse.

> This is my beloved
> and this is my friend.
>
> —Song of Solomon 5:16

Cheers for the Cook

What parent does not know the sinking feeling of sitting down to a well-thought-out and beautiful meal, only to hear one of the children say, "I don't like anything on the table"? Macaroni and cheese was his favorite food last week. And since when did she quit liking applesauce?

I guess it's not as bad as what I heard the neighbor boy say last week when his mom called him to dinner. "I don't like anything you're going to make."

I try not to take it as a personal insult when I'm the cook and my child is the impossible-to-please. I have thought of a way to restore the atmosphere, whether everyone's happy about the food or not. We will begin every meal with, "Three cheers for the cook!"

God, help me to know that I'm respectable,
whether or not the fruit of my labor
is appreciated.

Does not the ear test words as the palate tastes food?
With God are wisdom and strength.

—Job 12:11, 13

Serendipity

Last night my children were in a silly mood, which is quite ordinary. It's also gotten to be an ordinary event for Jonathan to spill his milk all over himself, his chair, and the floor. In the next minute, however, when he spilled a box of Styrofoam peanuts on the floor, I was not laughing. Determined to stay in control of myself, I calmly repeated my earlier request that he just go feed the hamsters.

He said, "Sure Mom," and happily swung the sack of corn and seeds over his shoulder. But the bag wasn't closed, and Jonathan's third mess was in the making.

He offered to help me clean everything up just as I was considering an offer to help him! As I bent over with the dustpan and brush, Jonathan jumped on my back, grabbing me tight around the neck. Now I was at my breaking point.

I had my mouth open, ready to yell, when he said, "Hugs, Mom. You need twelve a day," and proceeded to squeeze me twelve times. I began to soften, but when he asked if I would give him his twelve, my love for the spunky little boy was rekindled and burned bright.

**To act on love, even against one's will,
invites the feeling to come along, too.**

If you direct your heart rightly,
you will stretch out your hands toward him.

—Job 11:13

Child's Play

We had planned to be on the road by three o'clock, but it seemed like one child or the other was unpacking faster than I was putting things in. My impatience was mounting, but suddenly, instead of exploding, I was saved by a memory from my childhood.

I remembered that right before our family got in the car for the four-hour trip to Grandpa and Grandma's, my mother would sit all five of us around the table with a box of Cheerios and some string. We thought we were making necklaces so we would have an ever-ready snack on the road. Now I realized this was also Mother's scheme to keep us busy while she packed.

The only problem this time was that after I knotted Cheerios onto the ends of their strings, it all looked like so much fun, I kept stringing until I had a necklace, too. We still left later than we had planned. My attitude, however, had improved by indulging in play from my childhood for a few minutes.

**Engage yourself in some child's play
and capture your kids' unadulterated joy as well.**

Truly I tell you,
whoever does not receive the kingdom of God
as a little child will never enter it.

—Mark 10:15

School Days

I was prepared for the mixed emotions of having both my children in school. I would miss being with them, but I would also enjoy the returned freedom of time alone. Both happened accordingly.

What I didn't expect was that I would stay as busy as ever. Those big chunks of freedom closed up like quicksand. I could run my errands faster alone, so I filled up the leftover time with doing extra ones. My single friends started to invite me out for lunch again, and since I didn't need to get anyone home for a nap, I would stay with them most of the afternoon. I jumped onto the neighborhood committee to welcome newcomers and took on more responsibilities at church.

I have so much more time now and fewer reasons to decline requests for it. I have time to make meals for people who are sick and having babies and—I still don't have time to clean my house.

**How to fill my time
with what's most important
is a decision
I have to make continually.**

For everything there is a season . . .
a time to seek, and a time to lose;
a time to keep, and a time to throw away.
—Ecclesiastes 3:1, 6

Extracurricular

Along with the increased freedom I have, now that my children are in school all day, comes a new responsibility in my job description: taxi driver. Jonathan came home extremely excited because people can be on teams to do the things he loves: kick a ball, dribble a ball, throw a ball, bat a ball, and chase each other for the ball! Maria has discovered after-school art classes and writing labs. Both have heard that they can learn how to play the flute and the piano for just a little money, assuming we're paying, of course. Activities at church abound for school-age children, as well.

What good parents would deprive their children of every possible enrichment? Today, after driving from one thing to the other, to the other, to the other, with fifteen minutes squeezed in at home for supper, I don't even want to hear that question.

It is never enough
until you decide that it is!

All streams run to the sea,
but the sea is not full.

—Ecclesiastes 1:7

Loosen the Grip

I have a friend who experiences her greatest stress when her mother comes to visit. In fact, I have more than one friend who would admit to that.

It makes me wonder what kind of a mother my children will think I am when I want to spend a weekend with my children, in-laws, and grandchildren.

I don't have to wait that long to know. I can become alert right now to how comfortable my children are being with me. Even though they are still young and don't have much of a choice about my presence, are there ways I can loosen my grip of control? How can I show them that I respect who they are choosing to become?

**God, help me to know when to play
a strong part in shaping the lives of my children
and when to relinquish some of that directing
so they can choose the shape they will grow into.**

On you I was cast from my birth,
and since my mother bore me
you have been my God.

—Psalm 22:10

Continue to Loosen

Loosening the grip of control on my children is a continual process. The first time I left my baby with a childcare provider was the hardest. Ever since then I've tried to take additional steps toward letting them experience more of life than I can provide. Each loosening is painful.

They went to the Sunday School class for two-year-olds, where someone else taught them about faith. They began playing at friends' houses where other parents influenced them and they discovered different lifestyles, rules, and toys. Now they are in school where friends and teachers about whom I know little fill a main role in their development.

I will have many more chances to let go of my control so they can learn from others. I'm guessing that these steps which seem huge are only practice hops preparing me for the big ones yet to come.

**God, help me trust those
who share in the raising of my children.
Give me wisdom to know whom
I should not trust.**

But let all who take refuge in you rejoice;
let them ever sing for joy.
Spread your protection over them,
so that those who love your name may exult in you.

—Psalm 5:11

Bored?

When I first heard my daughter say she was bored, I ignored her. I thought she was too young to know the meaning of the word. The next time she said it I asked her what it means to be bored. I was wrong. She knows.

I immediately tried to fix it for her with my suggestions. She could help me make supper or clear the table. She could practice her flute, rake leaves, or play a game with her brother. I soon recognized the futility of my attempts. When a child is bored, nothing a parent comes up with will fill the gap. I finally told her that boredom is something that happens inside her, and she would have to choose what to do about it. She found a book to read.

**Lord, help me not to waste energy
doing things my child needs to learn
how to do for herself.**

You will forget your misery;
you will remember it as waters that have passed away.
—Job 11:16

Building Creativity

When Maria's dad heard that she's been saying she's bored, he said he couldn't be happier. I, protective Mother Hen, couldn't believe what I was hearing and needed further explanation. He said a lot of children never have time to be bored. They are given activities and events that fill up every minute of their days. They rarely have time to be alone and think about what they most want to do. He thinks it's great that Maria has time to be bored and is confident that she will make good use of it.

**Creativity and strength
are built by having time to discover
what's inside one's soul.**

They shall obtain joy and gladness,
and sorrow and sighing shall flee away.

—Isaiah 51:11

Trust

"Where are we going, Mom?" The question from the backseat of the car caught me off guard.

"Didn't I tell you, I'm taking you to Eric's house to play while I go to the dentist?" I thought I had told him. I've had it on my calendar for a week. I've had it on my mind all morning while prodding him to move at a more rapid pace than usual, trying to get out of the house on time.

Now as I peek at him in the rearview mirror, I'm amazed at his trust in me and his easy adjustment to my plans for his day. He's not a baby anymore, whom I can bundle up and carry everywhere with no explanation. He has become a little boy with his own thoughts and feelings about how to use his time. It's time I put some extra energy into respecting this admirable trust.

**Help me, O God,
to deserve the trust my children
give so freely to me.**

Many proclaim themselves loyal,
but who can find one worthy of trust?

—Proverbs 20:6

Hurt Feelings

I'll never forget the sadness I felt the day my daughter walked away from a party and asked me for the car keys. She said all her friends had someone else to play with and the others wouldn't let her play with them. She wanted to read a book until it was time to leave.

I wanted to tell those kids that they weren't being nice. I wanted to tattle to their mothers who I knew would make them play with my child. I wanted to hug my daughter so long and hard that nothing and no one else would matter to her. I wanted to save her from rejection. But I knew I couldn't.

It's hard to watch my children's feelings being hurt. It's worse than being hurt myself. It's hard to know I can't fix their pain for them. I can't make the world be fair to them. The emotional exhaustion I experience when I can't protect my children, equals the physical exhaustion I felt when I used to care for them more fully.

Pray that your children's hurts
will make them kinder to others.

For the hurt of my poor people I am hurt,
I mourn, and dismay has taken hold of me.

—Jeremiah 8:21

Compassion

Last night I felt like I was going to explode. I have too many things to do and no clear plan about how or when I will get everything done. On top of that, both my kids are sick.

Besides my own stress, I have a friend whose mother just died. Another is waiting for a doctor's report on the tests she had done last week. My friend who was diagnosed with cancer had her first chemotherapy treatment and is feeling weak and nauseated. I want to make dinner for her family tonight, but I can't figure out what to make for my own family. My sister turns forty this week, and I haven't been able to think of what to send her to show how much I love and celebrate her life!

Last night when I felt an explosion coming, I went to bed. Morning gives me new hope to try again. I have to learn how to be compassionate—to hold my pain and the pain of the world, without letting it in so far that it destroys me.

**Lord, help me learn the differences
between caring for people
and taking care of them.**

Relieve the troubles of my heart,
and bring me out of my distress.

—Psalm 25:17

Give Yourself Credit

There's another piece to the puzzle of being compassionate in a world that can quickly suck me dry—being able to recognize what I am doing. When I feel overwhelmed with all the problems within me and around me, I tend to focus on all the things I'm not doing to help. I quickly discount the phone calls I make to ask how friends are doing, the cards of encouragement I write, the birthdays I do remember. I think more easily about the notes I didn't write, the gifts I didn't buy, the rooms I didn't clean.

A friend told me today that I do a lot for others. I said I had a hard time believing that. Then I realized that I am missing the ability to see me like she sees me, to notice when I do meet the needs of others.

**Look at yourself from across the table
and notice all you do
for your family, friends, and neighbors.**

My eyes are ever toward the LORD,
for he will pluck my feet out of the net.
—Psalms 25:15

Awareness

I made myself sit down today. I brewed a cup of my favorite tea, took it outside, sprawled out in a hammock chair, and let myself be held by its gentle sway. At first I was distracted by a sense of urgency about all that needed to be done in the house, the weeds in my flower beds, the voices of my children playing. Then I sank back and looked up at the blue sky with white clouds floating between the leaves of our hickory tree. Slowly the busyness in my mind began to fall away. Nothing seemed more important than absorbing the beauty of the moment.

This is what I need to take inside of me to revitalize my compassion. I need to be as gentle with myself as the soft, warm wind blowing towards me. Whatever else I most need to do will fall into place. Looking at the heavens, I'm sure of it.

Let the sky speak to you.

I look at your heavens,
the work of your fingers . . .
O Lord, our Sovereign,
how majestic is your name in all the earth!

—Psalm 8:3, 9

The Mean Parent

"I hate being the mean parent." Jeanine was describing how she feels as the parent who is responsible for her children most of the time. "I'm the one who helps them learn limits and responsibilities. I say, 'No more TV.' I say, 'Do your homework.' I make them do chores.

"Their father waltzes into their lives every couple of months with all kinds of toys and fun outings, trying to make up for the time he doesn't spend with them. So, of course, they see him as the fun parent, and, when they are upset with me, the one who proves his love.

"I'm sure when they're older they'll understand how much love I give to them by being present and by providing stability. I know that in my head, but it hurts my heart to hear the kids refer to me as the 'mean parent.'"

**When raising children,
it's helpful to focus on a bigger goal
than ensuring their happiness
every moment of today.**

Teach me your way, O LORD,
and lead me on a level path.

—Psalm 27:11

Manners

It's hard to know when to enforce my children's practice of manners. I've insisted that they say Please and Thank You ever since they started talking, but other do's and don'ts aren't as clear to me.

I found myself being really angry at my child today when an adult asked her a question, and she just looked at him and then walked away. She does that to me sometimes, too, which I don't like, but I was downright chagrined when she did it to someone else.

I guess it's never too early to teach good manners to my children. I just have to know that they will likely need many, many reminders. My daughter doesn't yet seem to understand the need to answer questions she apparently considers unimportant.

I better reserve my "anger energy" for "long-haul energy."

**Adults don't always have
an immediate response either.**

But as for me,
my prayer is to you, O Lord.
At an acceptable time, O God,
in the abundance of your steadfast love,
answer me.

—Psalm 69:13

Old Enough?

I am so tired of getting up in the middle of the night, dragging myself upstairs to accompany my son from his room to the bathroom, waiting at the door, and then tucking him back into bed. He's old enough to do that alone.

Remembering his interest in money, I came up with a great plan. I told him I'd give him a nickel for every time he got up at night and went to the bathroom by himself, without yelling for me. I wasn't really sure it was the greatest idea. I could just see him keeping track in college and making me pay up at Thanksgiving break.

I needn't have worried. Without a minute's hesitation, he said, "I don't need any more nickels." When I recovered from my shock, my first impulse was to raise the reward. Maybe he doesn't have enough dimes. My second thought was, "I guess he still needs me."

**My children may define "old enough"
differently than I do.**

Attend to me, and answer me;
I am troubled in my complaint.

—Psalm 55:2

One, Two, or More

"I don't see how you do it with two children." Ann was commenting about my day's schedule of activities. "I feel like my head's twirling to keep up with one," she went on. "I can't imagine having a second."

It's true that my two children have many different interests and sometimes have to be on opposite sides of the city at the same time. But they often play well together, which makes it easier than having just one child. They play baby puppy together much better than I could or would as a partner.

What I can't figure out is how Lily and Randall do it with three or Kathleen and Bill with four, or any family where parents are outnumbered by children. We are all baffled to think about the number of children in our grandparents' families. Considering them makes me realize that I could be more tired than I am. Is that comforting?

Give thanks for the size of your family
as you ask for patience and wisdom
to keep it functioning!

I will appoint Peace as your overseer
and Righteousness as your taskmaster.

—Isaiah 60:17

Finding a Balance

There has to be a balance between letting my child choose everything she wants to do and still exposing her to all the available religious and cultural events I'd like her to enjoy. I clearly haven't found that critical point yet.

Last night as the grand finale to Maria's birthday festivities, I reserved a seat for her at the concert where my chorus was singing with our city's symphony. What I imagined to be an inspiring and enriching evening for her, turned out to be an expensive nap. She was too worn out to appreciate the gift that I gave, more from my desire for her than from her own interest.

**Consider your child's interests
and energy level
before imposing your own.**

It is not good to eat much honey.

—Proverbs 25:27

Stretch

Sometimes when I'm caught in fatigue and stress I feel paralyzed by it. The mountain of responsibilities or chores or relationship-building I need to climb seems too high, so I just stay at the bottom.

This week I experienced enough grace to ask others what they do when they're worn out. Matt's technique was both simple and intriguing. He stretches, sometimes for an hour! Right, he doesn't have kids. What parent would have an entire hour to stretch?

On the other hand, what parent couldn't do it for shorter periods in the middle of an ordinary day? It seems simple. It's easy to do. It feels good. It releases tension. The hard part is remembering to do it.

Go ahead.
Stretch while you read today's scripture.
Let your tension
shoot right out from your fingertips.

I am poured out like water,
and all my bones are out of joint;
my heart is like wax;
it is melted within my breast.

—Psalm 22:14

Homework

I like to be as supportive of my children's teachers as possible. Sometimes, however, the hours I spend helping with homework cut deeply into my family plans for the evening. I know school is my kids' job by the time they're old enough to go. Do they have to bring their work home, though? Isn't six hours of work enough for young children?

This is a conflict for me. I'm glad for good teachers and want to respect their judgment. I also want my children to have plenty of unstructured time to allow their personalities and imaginations to grow.

It would not be helpful for me to let my children know about my struggle. If I let my frustrations show, it would only fuel their own. Their energy needs to be spent, instead, on learning to study and make good use of their time.

**My children need to know my support,
not my frustration.**

Be strong,
and let your heart take courage,
all you who wait for the LORD.

—Psalm 31:24

Teach Study Habits

Perhaps my own uncertainty about homework is why I sometimes have so little patience when helping with it. When my child whines and complains about an assignment, I'm tempted to whine back and say, "Just do it," or some other similar unhelpful comment. We both want it to be over, yet it easily escalates into a battle between us.

What would happen if we would team up on the same side? If I asked how I can help instead of throwing my demands on top of her already existing frustration? Could I use this as a chance to teach my child some of the ways I've learned to manage stress: breathe deeply, do the hardest work first, plan rewards, recognize the progress I've already made, set the timer and see how much concentrated work I can do in a limited amount of time.

God, help me be creative
in finding the best way
to help my child learn to study.

Make your face shine upon your servant,
and teach me your statutes.

—Psalm 119:135

Set Up Rewards

Every child is different, but tonight I found a way that rewarded Maria for homework success. When she pulled out her math book (the dreaded *M* word), I set a cup of frozen blueberries in front of her. I told her she could eat a blueberry after each problem she completed.

What a pleasant surprise! Instead of going into the preliminary panic that the math book usually sets off, she started right in on the first problem. When she needed help from me, we both got a blueberry after successfully completing a problem.

While I don't want to set up food as the ultimate reward, it worked for us this time. She felt the pride of completing math in less time than usual. Now we'll work toward completing an assignment as sufficient reward in itself.

Honor your children's accomplishments.
Remember that they are of
greater importance to them
than your adult lenses may show.

You have turned my mourning into dancing;
you have taken off my sackcloth
and clothed me with joy.

—Psalm 30:11

Homeschooling?

As I struggle with homework battles and tired children, I hear the voices of my acquaintances who homeschool their kids. "If you struggle so much with traditional education, do it yourself." "If you do homeschooling, you can study the subjects that are harder in the morning while they're more alert." "With one-on-one attention, children can learn in less than half the time. Then they have plenty of free time."

They have some convincing arguments, and I admire every parent I know who homeschools. I've thought about it, but it's not right for me. I would be a much less patient and loving mother if I were also my children's teacher. Instead, I'll help their professional teachers as much as possible. I'm glad my homeschooling friends respect my decision.

**Lord, help me always to make the best choices
and to respect others who choose differently.**

I am your servant;
give me understanding.

—Psalm 119:125

Self-Determination

"You didn't ask me if I want a blueberry bagel for breakfast!" Jonathan wailed as I set before him the same breakfast he had been eating for weeks.

"I'm sorry," I replied. "Did you want something different this morning?"

"No, but I might want cereal sometimes." He's right, of course. He wants to be asked and he deserves to be.

That complicates my life slightly, since it's easier for me to do things the way I've always done them. Especially when I'm tired, I like doing what's automatic in my brain.

Jonathan's demand for self-determination reminds me of his dad. After eighteen years of knowing him, I still won't tell a hostess what he wants in his coffee. He likes to be unpredictable, so I never know what he will choose.

I may be watching a boy growing up to be like his dad. It takes a lot of energy to let these guys stay out of the slots I would put them into.

Keep me aware, Lord,
of the choices I can give my child.

Do not provoke your children to anger,
but bring them up in the discipline
and instruction of the Lord.

—Ephesians 6:4

From Anger to Sadness

I'm grateful tonight for a sense of well-being. This morning I feared it would be impossible to retrieve it any time soon. I felt like the squirt gun I keep on the counter to remind the cat I don't like him sprawling on the table. I wasn't filled with harmless water, though; I was loaded with anger, ready to shoot at anyone who came close.

At the same time, I was on the verge of crying. When John had the compassion to ask me what was wrong, I melted into tears. I didn't really know.

So, I sat down and began writing in my journal. I wrote one thing I knew I was angry about, and then, one after another, people and incidents rolled out of my pen. As my anger splattered out onto paper, what I had left within was a lump of sadness. That I can live with peaceably.

**Help me, Lord,
to contain my sorrow.**

You gave me room when I was in distress.
Be gracious to me, and hear my prayer.

—Psalm 4:1

From Sadness to Anger

Anger is a strange thing. It creeps inside me as some benign emotion when I'm not paying attention, walks right over any sadness I might be carrying, and explodes it all into flames. Sometimes the fire burns within and I'm able to contain the anger. Sometimes it comes out and singes the people to whom I am the closest.

If I could recognize my sadness and allow myself to face it and understand it, could I prevent it from starting to smolder and then developing into anger? Or when I'm downright angry, could I quiet things by pausing to reflect about what sadness tripped off my furor?

Sometimes I'm too tired to figure it all out. I have a hunch, however, that when I ignore my underlying stress, I keep the flames alive. If I can turn a little more energy toward what's really bothering me, the brushfire will die down and I'll be able to see the sadness for what it is—painful and wearisome, but not necessarily destructive.

When anger gets a hold on me, O God,
give me the energy to see what lies at its roots.

Hear, O LORD, when I cry aloud,
be gracious to me and answer me!

—Psalm 27:7

Sex or Not?

The first thing I let go when I'm tired is exercise. Following at a close second is sex. It's not that I decide to delete those things from my life; it just happens. If I were making conscious decisions, they would be two things I would definitely keep. Exercise keeps my body healthy; sex reminds me of the goodness of our marriage and the love we have to give each other.

Some say that sex is the barometer of a relationship. Usually I'm too tired to even think about looking at the barometer. I'm lucky if I remember our goodnight kiss after my head hits the pillow.

Before we had children, sex was a pleasure that happened spontaneously. Maybe that's why it seems improper to plan it now. On the other hand, our choice now seems to be—plan it or it won't happen.

Planned sex may not feel spontaneous enough.
Considering the alternatives
at this weary point in your life,
it may not be a bad idea.

Upon my bed at night
I sought him whom my soul loves.
—Song of Solomon 3:1

Planned Sex

Planning for sex is harder than it sounds. I can plan for it all day, then be so tired by the time the kids are in bed that my plans don't seem important at all—if I even remember I planned.

It's hard not to consider the clock. If I see that it's late, I don't think about whether I have energy left now; I think about how many hours are left before the alarm goes off in the morning. I'm suddenly planning how to reserve every bit of energy for what the next day will bring.

Even with the best-laid plans, our children's sleep schedules are still so irregular that the inspired moment is often lost to interruptions. Late-night phone calls can be plan-eliminators, too. I can't remember how many times one of us has fallen asleep waiting for the other one to get off the phone. What ingredient am I missing?

If your best-laid plans for intimacy are foiled,
consider what needs to change.

My dove, in the clefts of the rock,
in the covert of the cliff,
let me see your face,
let me hear your voice.

—Song of Solomon 2:14

Making Love

I had one of those dreams again last night about an old boyfriend. As usual, I was getting ready to marry him and wondered why I wasn't marrying John, since I loved him more. I woke up, relieved to see John sleeping beside me. These dreams usually indicate that something's missing in our lovemaking.

I thought back to the early years of our marriage. Nothing mattered to either of us more than being together. We loved talking and walking and eating together. We loved sleeping next to each other and waking up in the same bed. We were each other's priority. We would not allow our intimacy to be interrupted—by the phone, by time constraints, or by friends.

If we can't manage to avoid all interruptions, we can renew our lovemaking by imagining that this is the first time we've ever touched each other.

Make love again for the first time.

> You are altogether beautiful, my love;
> there is no flaw in you.
> —Song of Solomon 4:7

Telemarketers

When the phone rings at 6:00 p.m. and the voice doesn't sound familiar, I prepare for a very short conversation, ending with, "No thanks. I'm not interested." Depending how my day is going, I find a less polite way of saying the same thing. If the unfamiliar voice can't pronounce my last name correctly, I'm sure it's a telemarketer and I feel like hanging up immediately. The only thing that disgusts me more than someone trying to sell me one more credit card in the middle of my dinner is when they call me as I'm rushing to get the food on the table.

One never knows, though. Tonight, at exactly 6:00 p.m., the phone rang; the voice was unfamiliar and pronounced my name wrong. It was only by God's grace that I wasn't rude. The woman at the other end was my new neighbor from Kenya. She was calling to thank me for the housewarming gift I had earlier given to her husband! I was left shaking, thinking about what I might have said.

**Thank you, God,
for the miracle of keeping my mouth shut
this time.**

Do not neglect to show hospitality to strangers,
for by doing that some have entertained angels
without knowing it.

—Hebrews 13:2

Moving

I have moved to different homes about twenty times in my life, but this move is the hardest one yet. Our family is planning to leave the city where we've lived for eighteen years. We're going to another state and into the country. But the hardest part is the Child Factor.

This is the only home our children have ever known. Here live the friends with whom they have done and learned everything. How can they know there are other fun and beautiful places to live? How can I assure them that they will make new friends as good as the ones they have now? How can I convince them that they will also be happy in a different house?

I can't. That is the painful part of this move. They will eventually learn all these things themselves. For now, though, I have to hold the goodness of our decision in my heart, for me and for them.

**Help me, Lord,
to bear the weight
of what I cannot explain to my children.**

You shall see,
and your heart shall rejoice.

—Isaiah 66:14

November 29

Another holiday has come and gone and I didn't decorate for it. I did get the box marked "Thanksgiving" out of storage, but there it sits in the living room, still unopened.

I didn't decide not to put the pinecone turkey on the table or display the cornucopia on the mantle. I just never got around to those details. By Thursday I was doing well to make my one dish of baked corn for the big dinner at my sister's house.

I believe in celebrating life. I'm also convinced that planning for those celebrations should be as life-giving as the events themselves. If I'm in a frantic, have-to-do-it mode, something of the celebration has already been lost.

I decided to relieve myself of decorating this year. Then I relaxed and enjoyed the holiday, especially being with my family. I can decorate another year.

**Reconsider the "shoulds"
to see if they are life-giving enough to do.**

Go, eat your bread with enjoyment,
and drink your wine with a merry heart;
for God has long ago approved what you do.

—Ecclesiastes 9:7

Frantic in December

Okay, so I missed one holiday. I don't want to skip the next one. How can I not feel like decorating for Christmas?

But that's exactly how I feel—like doing nothing. I'm so preoccupied with other things today that getting out the Advent box feels like too big a job. Christmas looms like a bowling ball, ready to knock down the insignificant little pins of activity I've begun to set up.

I feel that I must put out a big effort for this major event or we haven't had a proper Christmas. "Big Effort" is the last thing I have in me to give.

Sometimes when I feel a frantic need to do something I don't have energy for, the best thing I can do is go to bed. I think I will.

**Sometimes I pray for energy to keep going;
sometimes for the ability to stop.**

I relieved your shoulder of the burden;
your hands were freed from the basket.

—Psalm 81:6

Listen to Your Body

I'm glad I listened to my weary body and went to bed when I couldn't imagine doing any creative planning for Christmas. The next day I woke up with a head cold. It may have developed into a worse one than it did, if I hadn't stopped pushing myself that night.

Today I've been inspired and energized. I played Christmas music while I zipped around the house, and I got more decorating and planning done in two hours than I could have done in ten weary evenings of forced labor.

When I lose my energy, I get this gut-level fear that it will never return. My head should know by now that if I let my body rest when it requests to do so, it will make up for lost time.

Thank you, God,
for the cycles of energy.
Help me learn to honor them.

I know your rising up and your sitting down,
your going out and coming in.
—Isaiah 37:28

Advent

At least three catalogs arrive in the mail every day now, beside all the extra inserts in the newspaper. I have so many options for things to buy, crafts to make, recipes to serve, events to attend, get-togethers to plan. Too many options.

I was greatly relieved to find at the top of the Advent box, a paper I had forgotten all about. It was a list I made at the end of the Christmas season last year, detailing the things our family did to make the holidays meaningful. We have already begun some wonderful traditions, like fashioning an Advent wreath, making our favorite cookies, reading a little more of the Christmas story each day, and adding a straw to the manger (to make a soft bed for Jesus) for each good deed someone does.

I'm so grateful for that paper's reminder. I don't have to reinvent traditions every year, scouring the magazines for new ideas. I can always add a new activity or two as they come, but the wealth of the season will build on repeating what we've found most important.

**Record the traditions important to your family,
thus doing away with the need
to rediscover them each year.**

Stand firm and hold fast
to the traditions that you were taught.

—2 Thessalonians 2:15

Traditions

We have family traditions for all seasons of the year—and they bring us true pleasure over and over. We have two campgrounds that are "ours." We camp at one in the summer and the other in the fall. We rent an oceanfront room for a weekend getaway in the winter. In the spring, we always plant our regular flowers and vegetables, as well as something new.

As the children grow older, they anticipate traditions and grow into new aspects of each one. They crowed about being big enough to go to the campground bathhouse alone for the first time. Each year they swim further out into the lake or hike further up the mountain. We plan with them and build new memories. We love watching them grow.

We've found a stability and ease in observing traditions as a family. Particular practices change over the years, but I doubt they will be forgotten.

**Thank you, God,
for being the foundation
of all our plans and activities.**

The LORD is exalted . . .
he will be the stability of your times.

—Isaiah 33:5–6

Throw Away

Some of my children's artwork hangs on the refrigerator and some covers the walls. Their crafts decorate every bookshelf and dresser top we own. I mail some of their pieces to the grandparents, aunts, and uncles.

Yet no matter how creative I am with dispersing their creativity, reams of their hard work remain in a very uncreative pile. I recently heard a helpful comment about such artwork. The process of doing art and crafts is important for children. Learning that has helped reduce my pile. I keep a few select examples of each child's work at various ages, file them into a marked folder, and pitch the rest. Now I just hope they don't ask me what happened to one specific project!

**When it's time to clean house
of your child's creations,
pray that the creative process
really was the most important part
and that they won't miss the rest.**

Listen to advice and accept instruction,
that you may gain wisdom for the future.

—Proverbs 19:20

Holiness

I love to watch my children sleeping. Noticing their peaceful relaxation is a holy moment for me.

Why do I go to such great lengths to keep myself from that same relaxation? I talk myself out of naps. I work through the evening until a late hour finally justifies bedtime.

Children live in a blissful state of not having to prove their worth. We love them for who they are more than for what they do.

I, on the other hand, seem to have this need, usually subconscious, to be productive. It's not enough to *be* any more. I have to do and do well.

What would happen if I allowed myself to be loved like I love my children—simply because I am? I bet I wouldn't be so worn out.

**Help me to love myself, Lord,
like you love me.**

But now thus says the LORD, . . .
I have redeemed you;
I have called you by name,
you are mine.

—Isaiah 43:1

Preoccupied

I don't have a problem like some parents do with tuning out my kids because I'm too involved in a television program or reading. In fact, I don't think I could ignore them if I tried when I'm concentrating on things outside myself.

Today, however, I find myself so involved within that I'm not listening to my children. I hear them talking and I respond on automatic. Emotionally, I'm with my friend who is sick. I want to be with her, but she lives too far away to run over for the day. She doesn't need me. She has other people with her. But I want to be with her to make sure she's being taken care of in the best way possible.

I feel torn by this thought and needing to take care of my children. I'm not being present for them either. While I'm not flying off to my friend's house, I'm preoccupied with her, to the exclusion of life where I am.

**God, it's so easy for me to get swallowed up
in caring about others.
Help me not to let that tendency
block my care of the ones
who are most completely depending on me.**

Let the words of my mouth
and the meditation of my heart be acceptable to you,
O Lᴏʀᴅ, my rock and my redeemer.

—Psalm 19:14

Selflessness

I'm home with a sick child again today. I should be glad to be here. I'm fortunate to have flexible work that allows me to be home with him. I have friends who not only have to find regular childcare, but also different childcare when their children are sick. They risk losing their jobs if they stay home too often with sick kids.

So, I grant that I'm fortunate to be able to rearrange my plans and allow Jonathan to stay in his own bed. I have to keep reminding myself of that, though, on this third day of providing sick care. I'm not feeling as empathetic with him anymore. In fact, I'm starting to feel sorry for myself.

I can usually manage the part of parenting that demands my selflessness. But it helps if I can complain about it sometimes.

**Thank you, God,
for accepting and strengthening me
when I begin to wallow in self-pity.**

My soul clings to you;
your right hand upholds me.

—Psalm 63:8

Keeping Secrets

When my friend asked me if I could keep secrets, I eagerly said, "Yes, of course!" I always like being let in on exclusive information.

What she said, however, made me sad. She is thinking about leaving her husband. She feels guilty about breaking her vows to him, so she doesn't want people to know her plans. She permitted me to tell my husband if I felt like I had to, but she preferred that I did not.

I thought, at first, that I didn't need to tell anyone. It isn't my secret, after all. The burden of knowing her pain, without being able to talk about it, has consumed more of my energy than I expected. Keeping secrets from the one with whom I share most of my life is too much to ask.

I will be more lenient, now, with the child who cannot wait with a birthday secret. It may be a sign that we belong together.

Help me discern, Lord,
when to keep confidences
and when I need to talk.

How precious is your steadfast love, O God!
All people may take refuge in the shadow of your wings.
—Psalm 36:7

God of the Little Things

I had an interesting discussion recently with the mother of a little boy who is developmentally delayed. I asked her where she gets the energy for all the extra doctor and therapy visits, besides the stress of wondering if her child will ever be able to live independently.

She said she doesn't believe there is a God who cares about her specifically. With all the big problems in the world, like whole countries living in the middle of war or starvation and the aftermath of natural disasters, how could there be a God who cares about her relatively small problems? Prayer seems like a waste of time. She prefers to receive the energy she needs from the goodness of the people who surround her.

I had no need to argue. I do, however, have an increased desire to let her experience God's love through my caring about her "little" problems.

**Think of yourself as an open channel,
receiving God's love
and then letting it flow through you
to your family and friends.**

Upon you I have leaned from my birth;
it was you who took me from my mother's womb.
My praise is continually of you.

—Psalm 71:6

Channel of Love

I spend most of my time with my children. How can I be a channel of God's love to them?

I am the one they will likely look to as they develop their image of God. If I love them and forgive them, they will understand God as loving and forgiving. If I consistently have too little or no time for them, they will experience a distant God.

God is not limited to the witness I give, thankfully. Their foundational concepts of God, however, will come through the channels I provide.

Don't be overwhelmed,
or take for granted,
the responsibility of being God's channel of love.

Just as you do not know
how the breath comes to the bones in the mother's womb,
so you do not know the work of God,
who makes everything.

—Ecclesiastes 11:5

How to Pray?

How small an item in my life does God care about? Am I wasting God's time when I ask for help in finding a parking space? Is "wasting God's time" an appropriate concept? Does God care about the head cold our family has been passing around for the last two weeks? Can I bother God to help me work out the details of a day I cannot see my way through clearly?

I asked a friend what she thought. She said she doesn't talk to God about the little things in life, but she believes that people who do are happier.

What could it hurt?

**Live for a day
as if God cares about
every little detail of your life.**

O Lord, all my longing is known to you;
my sighing is not hidden from you.

—Psalm 38:9

God, My Parent

My children help me immensely and indirectly as I think about my understanding of God. Wondering how much God cares about the details of my life reminds me of how much I care about my children.

When their feelings are hurt, I hurt with them. When they cry because of getting a shot, I wish I could have taken it for them. I hate to see them in pain. I delight in giving them their favorite foods. I'm pleased when I hear their giggles.

Could God be any less concerned for me than I am for my children? God, the ultimate parent, creates and sustains me.

**Thank you, God,
for the gift to know, and be known, by you.**

Even before a word is on my tongue, O Lord,
you know it completely.

—Psalm 139:4

PMS

I was complaining to John this week about my lack of energy and my more-than-usual irritation at everything. He said, "It's that time of the month, isn't it?"

It is that time of the month! Why can't I ever remember that? I've been living in this body that bleeds every month for many years, and I still refuse to acknowledge the symptoms that tell me my period's coming. I blame myself and try to figure out why I'm extra tired and nagging.

John has learned to recognize my days of stress better than I do, maybe because he honors my physical makeup while I continue to fight it. I don't want my energy and moods to be dictated by my body's functions.

I should know by now that resisting this situation takes more energy than accepting it. I will start marking my calendar so I can join my husband in knowing what's coming. He would probably appreciate the company.

**Give yourself the breaks
your body is asking for.**

You will increase my honor,
and comfort me once again.

—Psalm 71:21

Male PMS? Child PMS?

Do men have anything like PMS? Their bodies don't prepare monthly for the possibility of bearing a baby, but they must have cycles of energy, too. Might they also react with a fighting or denying impulse if they don't recognize those cycles?

Maybe children's bodies have cycles, too, beyond familiar daily needs for naps and bedtime. I can honor their need for increased sleep or time alone between periods of moving at full speed. I want to teach them to respond to the messages their bodies send.

It's an exhausting job to be aware of the whole family's cycles. Ignoring them, though is like getting hit by an unexpected wave at the beach. I'm surprised and then irritated. I prefer to watch the waves coming; then ride them in or dive through them.

When I honor myself,
I'm more likely to honor others.

O LORD, you will hear the desire of the meek;
you will strengthen their heart,
you will incline your ear.

—Psalm 10:17

Marble Method

How am I going to get my kids to be more responsible? I'm so tired of reminding them of the same tasks over and over! I feel like a nag and I can see them tuning me out. I yell louder, which usually gets a response, but then we all feel a few degrees worse. A simple chore, which I think should be routine, has become a source of conflict again.

After I spewed out all this frustration to John, he suggested that we try rewarding them for what they do rather than noticing all they don't do. So, we decided to make a list for each child, as simple as possible, of what we expect. Pictures will explain for the youngest. Then instead of repeated reminders, I can just say, "Have you finished your list?" When they complete their list, they can put a marble in the Reward Jar. When the Jar is full, we will plan a special activity to do together.

It sounds great in theory. I'll start by taking them shopping so they can each pick out their favorite bag of marbles. I'm getting revived just by planning a solution!

Think positively.

People will say,
"Surely there is a reward for the righteous."
—Psalm 58:11

Added Responsibility, Added Rewards

After our family got the marble plan rolling, we decided to attach an addendum. If the children do extra chores, they can put extra marbles in the Jar. We don't yet expect them to scrub the shower curtain or wash the windows as part of their routine chores. They are physically able to do those things, even if their "completed" job needs a follow-up touch. They can have the satisfaction of going beyond the requirements of living in this family.

I have to keep the goals clearly in mind to ensure that these plans are fair and fulfilling. The immediate goal is not to get my work done. (That is the long-term plan.) For now, however, I want the children to know they are an important and necessary part of this family. We appreciate their help, and we need them.

**Lord, help me to keep a good balance
between my expectations
and what my children have to offer as they grow.**

May the LORD reward you with good
for what you have done to me this day.

—1 Samuel 24:19

Subconscious Memories

I've discovered that I have few, if any, memories before I was six years old.

I was disappointed to discover that, not only for myself, but because I wonder if my children will remember any more than I have. They have had many people love and care for them and then move out of their lives before they turned six. (It's probably divine intent that they don't remember who all changed their diapers.) But we've had so many fun times with them that I wish they would remember.

When someone asked me how I think my parents felt when I was born, I had no doubt that they were totally delighted. All my conscious memories are built on a solid subconscious foundation of being loved.

That's what I have to give to my children as well. I know every loving thing I do for them becomes part of who they are, whether or not they remember the details.

**Take pictures as you can afford them,
journal as you are able,
trust the rest to the accumulation of full love.**

Save your people, and bless your heritage;
be their shepherd, and carry them forever.

—Psalm 28:9

What, Really, Do I Think?

"What will the neighbors think?" I hated when my parents said that to my siblings and me when we were little, especially when we were only pretending to be angry with each other.

Imagine my surprise when I heard myself saying that very thing to my children today. They weren't pretending, though. When they kept fighting over toys in the sandbox, I imagined my neighbors listening and thinking, "What nasty kids that woman has! Can't she control her own children?"

Now that I've had the benefit of reflection, I wish that my first thought had been how to help them reconcile their differences instead of worrying about what the neighbors would think.

I can't take care of the whole world. It's a big enough job to nurture and care for this small piece of it.

Lord, help me speak peace to my children
for the good of our family,
not what I imagine others' standards to be.

Do not remember the sins of my youth
or my transgressions;
according to your steadfast love remember me,
for your goodness' sake, O Lord!

—Psalm 25:7

Parenting as Parented

When I hear a tape from my childhood come flowing unconsciously out of my mouth at my own children, I realize how much my parenting is affected by how I was parented. A LOT! From what kind of cookies I bake most often to how I discipline my kids, I find it easiest to repeat the actions and responses with which I was raised.

When I decide I want to do something different from my parents, I must exert much more effort. When I'm tired, that's almost impossible!

Help me, Lord,
both to maintain the goodness of my heritage
and to uphold decisions
about how I want to change.

Restore to me the joy of your salvation,
and sustain in me a willing spirit.

—Psalm 51:12

Who's Tired of Whom?

I was aware of Jonathan's presence as I was doing the dinner dishes. I was simply aware, but no more. He stood quietly beside me, allowing me to stay deep in my own world of thought, until . . . "Didn't you hear me not talking?" Apparently, he could hold it no longer.

I wondered how long he had been practicing this utter self-restraint beside his oblivious mother. I was immediately grateful that he had finally expressed himself so I would know what he was doing with so much effort! I quickly bent down to give him a hug and find out what else he was thinking.

I will never know everything that's happening inside my child. I need these occasional reminders that I sometimes wear him out as much as he wears me out.

**Lord, give my children patience
to live with their parents.**

For with you is the fountain of life;
in your light we see light.

—Psalm 36:9

Growing Old Gracefully

Since we live two hundred miles from our children's closest grandparent, we decided to adopt "Grandma" Clarice and "Grandpa" Waverly, who live near us. We met them just before our first child was born, when they were seventy years old.

John and I knew they were special from the first time we met them. Even though they each have had health problems, that is never the first topic of discussion. They answer our inquiries about their health, but quickly move on to ask about our lives.

They have become as important to our children as they are to us. They never tell the children to calm down in their house full of breakable things. They take Maria and Jonathan to McDonald's and actually eat with them. They come to our house and don't complain about crawling onto our picnic table's backless benches. They always supply the Cokes and potato chips.

If I want to be this much fun to be around when I'm eighty, I better start living that way now.

**Be the kind of friend
you enjoy being with.**

Your life will be brighter than the noonday;
its darkness will be like the morning.

—Job 11:17

Cat's Life

Sometimes I'm really jealous of our cat. He has nothing to do all day but curl up in a sunny spot and sleep. If anyone bothers him, he just wanders to another cozy spot. He exists mostly for himself and has most of his needs met. He officially belongs to my daughter who adores everything he does, from sleeping with her in bed, to jumping at specks of dust.

I wonder how long I'd be content to do only what I want to do, to live for no one but myself. I may think I'd enjoy having others care for all my needs, but I'd soon tire of not having control. I thrive on being surrounded by people who need me. I grow by trying to cheer up the world around me.

I wouldn't want to be a cat, but I could use one catnap in the sun right now.

**God, when I get tired
of taking care of my children,
help me remember the cat alternative—boring!**

My help comes from the LORD,
who made heaven and earth.

—Psalm 121:2

Be

A lesson from the cat—he does not have to do anything special to be loved. He's loved just because he's our cat.

Maybe there's some place between the lay-around cat pace and the crazy rat race I often live in that would be more ideal. When I quiet myself and just be for a while, I realize how exhausting doing is. Am I really trying to prove that my existence is worthwhile? Or do I have a deep-down fear that if I stop, rest, and be, I might never get up and do anything again?

Those are all pretty silly motivators. Doing will always be natural. Being is what I have to be deliberate about.

Consider, in the quiet of your soul,
how valuable you are,
just because you were created.

Judge me, O LORD,
according to my righteousness
and according to the integrity that is in me.
—Psalm 7:8

Stimulated

Now that Molly's children are both in school, her husband thinks she ought to do something with the master's degree she earned ten years ago. Her first love, though, is still to be with her children. If they're at school, that's where she wants to be. Laminating, cutting out pictures, putting up bulletin boards, whatever the teachers need to have done, that's what Molly will do. If they don't keep her busy enough, she goes home to make cookies for her children's classes or buys them all popsicles when it's hot.

I carry on the same conversations within that Molly has with her husband. Are these menial tasks too far beneath my training, less than what I have to offer the world? And is it enough that our children keep us emotionally stimulated, if not intellectually invigorated?

**Priorities come from within,
not from comparing myself to another person
or to a different time in life.**

Do you not know that your body
is a temple of the Holy Spirit within you,
which you have from God,
and that you are not your own?

—1 Corinthians 6:19

Yo-Yo

I feel like a yo-yo. I can be happy and content with how many things are wonderful about life as I know it, and the next minute, one demand later, I am irritated and cranky.

One little smile and the cock of my daughter's head as she looks at me, and I'm cheered up, remembering the goodness of the moment. It fades quickly, though, when the phone rings and I find I have an extra meeting this week that I forgot about and don't want to go to.

My son stands beside me and says, "I love you," and I know that one extra meeting isn't the end of the world. Let him forget to close the door and my gentle reminders get grumpier.

My social work friends would tell me to see a doctor and get myself on some medicine for mood swings. I know what the real problem is. I'm exhausted!

I count myself fortunate
if the string on my yo-yo keeps bouncing me up
to see the beauty of life.

The LORD is the strength of his people;
he is the saving refuge of his anointed.

—Psalm 28:8

Look!

I felt my son come and stand close to me, watching. I was in the kitchen, surrounded by piles of dirty dishes, groceries to put away, cookies in the making, and an overflowing basket of laundry on the back burner of my mind. He said, "So, Mom, what're we gonna do today?"

I was about to tell him all the things I had to do. I already didn't know, in the middle of the morning, how I would get it all done. By an act of God, I looked at the child before I spoke. Thank goodness I looked at him! His eyes were full of delight—and questions about how he could be with me. I saw then that the most important thing in the world was to do something right then with him. Did anything have to be done immediately? No, everything could wait.

I'm so grateful I looked at him today, because I don't always. How often have I been too busy to notice how loving and wonderful my child is?

**God, thank you for your nudge
that helped me really look at my son.**

Listen, you that are deaf;
and you that are blind,
look up and see!

—Isaiah 42:18

A Response That Soothes

Yesterday when I was given the grace to look my child in the eyes when he came to talk to me, I gave up what I was doing. I sat down to read to him. I wanted him to know he was more important than all my chores.

I was ready to give him the rest of my morning. My work was no longer paramount; my full attention was his. After reading two short stories, however, he was off to play by himself again. That's all he needed.

Too often I tell him, "I'm busy right now." Then he wants my time even more and turns into a demanding kid; insatiable, in my mind. All he usually needs is a short reassurance of my love.

God, help me to honor my child's small requests
before my resistance
helps them grow into huge demands.

You are precious in my sight,
and honored,
and I love you.

—Isaiah 43:4

True Friendship

I promised my friend a week ago that I would call her. I think about it every day, but always when I'm snuggled into a chair reading to one of the kids, or hurrying to pick up the groceries I need for the cookies I have to bake for the afternoon school party, or getting to the bank before it closes. By the time the kids are in bed, I have one little window of time from 9:00 to 9:30, before it feels too late to call anyone.

Couldn't I find one little block of time to make one little phone call to one good friend in one whole week? I feel terrible.

The next time I see her, I realize again why she's my friend. When I apologize for my negligence, she just laughs and says, "That's okay, I didn't have time to call you either!"

**Surround yourself with friends
who don't demand an explanation
for that which cannot be explained.**

A true friend sticks closer
than one's nearest kin.

—Proverbs 18:24

Forgive to Grow

When I was a teenager, I remember being told that one job everyone has as they grow up is to forgive their parents. I was learning that all parents make mistakes and that we cannot change our past.

I'm remembering that advice on the evening of being a terribly imperfect parent. I yelled too much today. I was too strict in not letting Maria go to a friend's house. I made both kids go to bed early because I was too tired to absorb any more of their energy.

I'm sure I will do worse than this in the years to come—which makes me really tired. Who will tell my children that their job, in growing up, is to forgive me? Maybe they could hear it from my friend Bev. Then I'll return the favor and tell her children the same thing.

**Help your children relate to other adults
who may tell them things
they won't be able to hear from you.**

Be kind to one another,
tenderhearted,
forgiving one another,
as God in Christ has forgiven you.

—Ephesians 4:32

Discontent

When anyone asks me what I want for my birthday or Christmas, I have a hard time thinking of anything. Take me to a store, though, and I see all kinds of things I didn't know I needed. Let me go to a friend's house and I'm immediately noticing what they have that I'd like, too.

No wonder my children often want more toys or videos or computer games after they've played at a friend's house or seen commercials on TV. I get irritated about their constant begging in a store for the thing they've never seen before, but now can't do without.

Sometimes my refusal is not a matter of money. It's not that their desire is inappropriate. It's a matter of principle. We don't need a lot of things to be happy.

It takes more energy to teach them that principle than to give in to their pleas. If they learn it now, however, they'll be happier adults!

**I need to live the principles
I want my children to learn.**

I have learned to be content
with whatever I have.

—Philippians 4:11

Stages

One of the benefits of more and more years of parenting experience is that I am gaining perspective. I've seen enough stages come and go to know that when one comes along that's difficult, it won't last forever.

Sometimes I can't help protesting, like when they revert to baby talk at six years of age or talk back to me at any age. At other times, however, like when they insist on wearing the same shirt every day for months, or want exactly three songs sung to them at bedtime, I can indulge them.

I've learned that I can push hard, trying to expand their horizons at my pace, or let them move on when they are ready and save my energy for something more important.

**Learn to laugh at yourself
when a harmless stage drives you crazy.**

Strength and dignity are her clothing,
and she laughs at the time to come.
—Proverbs 31:25

Unwinding

I am always startled at how quickly my eagerness to be with my children can turn into complete frustration and anger. Some days I can hardly wait for school to be over so I can hear about their days and tell them about mine.

I pick them up, only to have them demand that we go to the video store immediately or beg to go to a friend's house. They won't accept my, "No," and soon start fighting over what music we'll listen to or who gets to sit where in the car.

I finally got brave enough to ask another mother if this ever happens to her. She laughed and said, "Sure. I figure they had to work hard at being good all day. They need to unwind, and they know they're safe enough with me to do it."

That was helpful, and it's true. Their teachers have never mentioned any behavior problems.

God, help me remember
that I will absorb more of my child's wrath
than anyone else,
because I am her safety net.

Uphold me according to your promise,
that I may live,
and let me not be put to shame in my hope.
Hold me up, that I may be safe.

—Psalm 119: 116–117

Empowerment

One family at my class reunion this weekend said they allow each child to plan and prepare one meal each week. The child makes the menu, helps buy the groceries, and does as much of the cooking as is age-appropriate—with the parents standing by as consultants.

What a great way to empower children. The responsibility allows them to go to the edges of their capacities, doing as much of the preparation as they are able or want to do. The "supervisors" can teach nutrition, the value of math for measurement, time management, and the ascetic value of mealtime. The kids can choose background music, a dinner grace, lighting, and conversation topics.

I can't wait to try it. I think for now I'll do the shopping myself. It's always more expensive with an extra set of hands deciding what we "need."

**Empowering children can be an asset
to the entire family;
in fact, to the world!**

God, our God, has blessed us.
May God continue to bless us;
let all the ends of the earth revere him.

—Psalm 67:6–7

More on Meals

My cousin breaks suppertime routine by inviting her kids to write creative suggestions for meals on slips of paper which they drop into a jar. On a certain night of the week, they choose one idea. They've tried using different-sized spoons and bowls than usual, sitting in a circle on the floor to eat, drinking from pint or quart jars, serving and eating each food in a different room of the house.

The ways to enliven dinner can be as creative as a family's imagination and as crazy as a parent's limits will allow. It sounds like a ridiculous thing for an already weary parent to add to an evening agenda. It may be the kind of activity, however, that adds energy with only a little extra effort.

**Lord, help me put an extra ounce
of energy into things
that will enhance our family's togetherness
in significant ways.**

Let the peoples renew their strength.

—Isaiah 41:1

Social Needs

"Don't come home until your social needs are met." That was John's loving advice to me as I headed out the door to a party. I had no one but myself to strap into a seat belt. What glorious freedom.

Before we had children, I gave little thought to the fact that I have more social needs than my husband. We did a lot of things together, and when he needed some alone time, I found other people to be with. I gave little thought to our separate comings and goings.

It's harder, now, for each of us to go off and find either more quietness or more interchange with others. That would mean leaving the other alone with the children. So we tend to go places together or stay home together. John must have realized I have some social needs that aren't being met within the confines of our family. He was rewarded, too. His gift of letting me go allowed me to gather the energy an extrovert gets from a crowd. I came home revitalized.

**Know and pursue
what gives you energy.**

They shall obtain joy and gladness,
and sorrow and sighing shall flee away.

—Isaiah 35:10

Second-Guessing

"Mom."

"Yes?"

I was met with a brief silence. Then, "What was I gonna think?"

I have often tried to figure out what my children are thinking, but I'm usually given a little more than this to go on!

I often assume I know what a simple statement means, only to find out I was way off. I thought that "I don't like this shirt" meant I may give it to her younger cousin, when it only meant she didn't want to wear it that day. I guessed that "I'm hungry" meant I better get home and make dinner, when he just had a hungry spot for that piece of candy he saw on the neighbor's table.

How often have I assumed I know what they're saying, and never find out how wrong I am? I probably don't want to know.

Children are ours, in part,
to keep us mindful
of the limitations of our humanity.

Blessed be the Lord,
who daily bears us up.

—Psalm 68:19

Words

I love words. I love to have words express what I'm feeling or thinking. I love to write them down for myself and for others. I love to talk and to hear what others say.

I have a child who seems to love words even more than I do. I have another child who seems to need them far less. Both extremes wear me out. I tire of listening to one and wish I knew what is inside the other.

I live best with both extremes when I'm centered myself, feeling compelled neither to talk nor to be silent. When I can accept myself, I can accept what my children have to give me as well.

Accepting myself,
I am better able to accept my children.

Hear my prayer, O God;
give ear to the words of my mouth.

—Psalm 54:2

Going in Circles

The washing machine has been broken for five days and they don't know when the part required to fix it will be in. Should I go to the laundromat or the store to buy more socks and underwear? I don't have time to do either.

My son has been excited ever since he found out that Clifford, the big red dog, will be at the Children's Museum tonight. My daughter wants to go to her friend's birthday party instead. They're both too tired to go anywhere!

It's also flu season, and this year's strain is especially wretched. Some people are having dangerous reactions to the flu immunization. My children have violent reactions to even thinking about receiving shots. I don't know what to do. Everyone from whom I seek advice gives me a different answer.

I finally have to make a decision and do it.

**Children, too, want someone to be in charge,
whether they admit it or not.**

From the end of the earth I call to you,
when my heart is faint.
Lead me to the rock that is higher than I.

—Psalm 61:2

Traveling

In our family, the parent who is most worn out gets to drive. The days of leisurely drives in the country or spontaneous visits to friends in the next state are over. Traveling with children is pure work.

I try to remember to go to the library for some new music or stories and to hide some new, fascinating snack close to their seats. Seat belts require a parent to be extra creative to help kids forget their confinement.

Traveling gets to be a pain in the neck, literally. I thought if I were asked (or told, rather) to turn around and look at one more thing today, my neck would never return to its normal position.

**It's easier to cope with stress
when I admit that it is real
and that I need help.**

Be gracious to me, O Lord.

—Psalm 9:13

Out of Control

"Mommy, why are you yelling so much?"

It was a simple question, spoken softly and innocently by my four-year-old. Its effect on me was like having my heart squeezed roughly into my stomach. Instantly, I felt terrible. And I stopped yelling.

I could tell him that everything he was doing was frustrating me. But that wasn't the real reason. I knew immediately that I was yelling because I was exhausted. In fact, anyone doing anything in my presence at this moment would irritate me.

I wasn't aware that I was yelling, but as his question hung in the air, I could see my rough voice reflected in his confused face.

He doesn't deserve this. No child deserves to be yelled at. I'm the parent and my son is more in control than I am. Lord, have mercy.

**Thank you, Lord,
for speaking to me through my child.**

No one can tame the tongue—
a restless evil, full of deadly poison . . .
with it we curse those who are made
in the likeness of God.

—James 3:8–9

Model Self-Control

My son taught me an unforgettable lesson when he calmly asked why I was yelling. If he would have yelled back, who knows how long I would have continued to find fault with everything he did.

I want to remember this moment also for those times in the future when my children will be in a similar state of exhaustion or fear. They, too, lash out under pressure. When I respond in the same tone and volume, it does little to stop or comfort them.

If I can guide them like my son helped me, they will more quickly learn self-control. If I can ask or question, rather than simply telling them to stop, they will learn to name their feelings. They will also know that someone loves them enough to look beyond the angry words to the pain inside.

**Flow through me, Lord,
to my children.**

My child, if your heart is wise,
my heart too will be glad.

—Proverbs 23:15

Satisfaction

Keeping a stockpile of toilet paper is not something I've ever heard mentioned in a list of accomplishments. Everyone takes that for granted, except the supplier. Children feel good when they learn how to take another roll out of the cupboard and mount it, but they don't have to worry about the supply being depleted. There are always more rolls in the closet.

Family life can go on when no one remembers to buy more milk. We'll have toast for breakfast. If we run out of potatoes, we change the menu. If we've used the last bar of soap, there's sure to be one of those miniature hotel bars in the suitcase. If there's no cleaning liquid left, no one minds postponing the task.

Toilet paper, though, is one item that's hard to do without. That explains my silent satisfaction when I replenished the TP—before anyone knew it was just in time. What a mom!

Give yourself credit
for every little accomplishment,
because it wouldn't be considered a small mistake
if you didn't do it.

A capable wife who can find?
She looks well to the ways of her household.

Proverbs 31:10, 27

Whom Does It Hurt?

I'm kind of jealous of the parents who can still lay out their children's clothes at night and know that's what they will wear the next day. If I did that, I'd ensure their refusal to consider what I chose. And so they wear the same things over and over, while all the outfits I would choose lie untouched at the bottom of the drawer.

I can usually accept their clothing choices, but today, in the heat of the summer, I could not talk Maria out of wearing her winter coat. She wasn't hurting anyone, so that's what she wore on our walk. Imagine my delight to see a mother walking toward us with a little girl who had at least thirty plastic barrettes in her hair! Now there's a good mother. She respects her child more than she cares about what any stranger on the street might think. I didn't really care anymore what anyone thought of the winter coat idea.

Lord, help me to grow in respect for my child.

You show me the path of life.
In your presence there is fullness of joy.

—Psalm 16:11

How Long Is Five Minutes?

My children are growing up with a warped idea of time. I blame them for not responding when I say, "Come," and not being ready when I say, "Let's go." But I'm as bad as they are.

I like to give them a warning when it's time to leave their friend's house, so I'll say, "We're going to leave in five minutes." Twenty minutes later I'm still talking to my friend, so I holler, "Two more minutes." Then I start moving toward the door, but, invariably, I miss the golden moment when my child has joined me because I've thought of one more thing I must say. And my child is off and playing again, sure that five minutes is a quite elastic amount of time.

**Pay attention to whatever
you want your children to pay attention to.**

The LORD is gracious and merciful,
slow to anger
and abounding in steadfast love.

—Psalm 145:8

Intentional Living

What if we could retire when we have children, and then, after they're grown and leave home, go back to our careers? Many people my age are raising young children while spending lots of time and energy at their jobs, earning enough to support themselves and their kids. We seem to want children, yet we're away from them a lot—so we can take care of them.

Many parents say that by the time they had time to be with their children, their children preferred to be with their peers. So when I am home with my kids, I want to be especially sensitive to their requests for my time and attention. Do the dishes really have to be done right now? Must I be on the committee I've been invited to chair? How important is it that I send birthday cards to all my friends?

**Lord, help me keep my children
on the top
of my list of priorities
whenever possible.**

Do not withhold good from those to whom it is due,
when it is in your power to do it.

—Proverbs 3:27

Feed Thyself

If my children are at the top of my priorities, and if I intend to be the best mother possible to them, I need to nurture my own soul. So I've joined a community chorus. I love to sing. I love practicing with a group. I love participating in concerts. And when I come home from singing, I hug my children with renewed passion.

One parent I know swims to feed her soul. Another takes art classes. Another finds time every day to play his piano.

When I'm already tired and haven't spent enough quality time with my children, it's not always wise to add one more thing to my schedule. But sometimes it is.

**If you are keeping your spirit alive and growing,
all those around you will be the benefactors.**

As a mother comforts her child,
so I will comfort you.

—Isaiah 66:13

Expecting Perfection

I always think it's such an inspired idea to make cut-out cookies with my children for special holidays. I did it with my family as a kid. So every Advent, Laurel and I make cookies with our children.

And every year I forget how frustrated I get doing it, until the first ball of dough gets rolled out and the first child slams the cookie cutter right in the middle. The first incident is not the problem. But after I explain to everyone four times about the importance of putting them close together, so we don't have to roll the dough out between every three cookies, I start getting upset.

Then the kids lose interest because Mom isn't fun anymore, and you can't ever do it well enough to please her anyway. Even if none of us says those things, they hang there in the air.

This year I will try again to remember that the children having fun is more important than perfect cookies. And I'll work with Laurel again, because another adult presence helps me to see that I'm taking the dough much too seriously.

**Children learn better by doing tasks
with encouragement
than by being told they're not good enough.**

Rash words are like sword thrusts,
but the tongue of the wise brings healing.

—Proverbs 12:18

Give It Up

I can be very compulsive. And that can interfere with letting my children be children. When Maria was planning her birthday party this year she saw a package of glittery confetti that she wanted to use in decorating. I finally bought it, but then went on to be very restrictive about how she scattered it across the tablecloth.

I explained to John apologetically that I had gotten it against my better judgment. "You're right," he said, "it's going to be all over the house." I thought he was being critical until he added, "And then we'll just clean it all up!"

My children are fortunate to have a father who is very different from their mother. Life is more fun for them.

**Just before you make a fuss about a mess,
put it in the perspective of eternal importance.**

"Martha, Martha,
you are worried and distracted by many things;
there is need of only one thing."

—Luke 10:41–42

Reset Buttons

A parent told me years ago that when she starts to get upset with her children, she asks herself if what they are doing will matter in ten years. If not, she tries to let it go. I'm practicing that question as a sort of reset button.

When I was about to scold my son for kicking his ball into the flowers yesterday, I remembered the ten-year question, reset my attitude, and enjoyed his athletic ability. When I felt my impatience rising this morning as I tried to get everyone out of the house, I asked myself how important two extra minutes are with a ten-year view.

Some things, like physically hurting others or out-of-control anger, need immediate correction. But most of what irritates me I can dismiss by activating my reset button.

**When exhaustion makes
coping with your children difficult,
find a reset button that works for you.**

The farmer waits for the precious crop from the earth,
being patient with it
until it receives the early and the late rains.
You also must be patient.

—James 5:7–8

Breaking the Speed Limit

If reset buttons help me to cope with my children's behavior, might such buttons assist me with my own? Here I sit at the end of the day, exhausted by having run from one thing to another, knowing I want to change something.

My friend Murray works with lots of smokers. When they take a smoke break, he matches that with a tea break. It's a calming ritual for him in the middle of a hectic executive's schedule.

A ten-minute midafternoon break might help me reset the speed at which I'm doing everything. I probably won't suffer from ten minutes of nonachievement as much as I'll benefit from refocusing my energy.

**Develop and then observe an afternoon ritual
that allows you to watch if you're
traveling at the right speed.**

You silence the roaring of the seas,
the roaring of the waves,
the tumult of the peoples.

—Psalm 65:7

Awareness That Sustains

I am sleep-deprived and I try to do too much, but being aware of the good things in my life sustains me. Concentrating on what goes wrong depletes me.

Today when I unexpectedly had several free hours, I pulled out an outfit Maria had been asking me to sew. When she tried it on, it was clear that it was fit only for the trash.

When I opened the Crock-Pot lid, the beans smelled too musty to eat. My soul dropped to my knees. Close to tears, I spotted four loaves of bread, cooling on the counter.

Supper was on time. We had homemade bread served with butter for the first course, honey on homemade bread for dessert, and I have been sustained.

Count on things going wrong.
Look for and celebrate what goes well.

Cast your burden on the LORD,
and he will sustain you.

—Psalm 55:22

Always a Parent

When I called my parents today to tell them about yet another ear infection for Jonathan, I learned they have plenty to worry about. My sister's youngest daughter had a tick bite and is starting daily injections for Lyme disease. My brother has passed his mononucleosis on to his wife and they're both too tired to care for their two little girls. My older brother and his wife worry about the friends their children are hanging out with in college. My other brother and his wife are expecting their first child—wonderful, but full of unknowns.

I decided not to invite my parents for the weekend to help us. They didn't say they are worn out, but they have to be. I don't believe my weary parenting will be over in eighteen years!

**Preserve me, Lord,
for the long haul!**

Even when you turn gray
I will carry you.

—Isaiah 46:4

About the Author

Sandra Drescher-Lehman enjoys being John's wife and partner and Maria and Jonathan's mother. After serving as a prison chaplain for ten years, she became a social worker in the field of mental health and then a pastor. Her greatest challenge is to find the best balance between busyness and being still. She lives in Souderton, Pennsylvania.